The Fourth Tier

AF073543

The Fourth Tier

Modernizing MTSS for Student Mental Health

Armand Pires

Ryan Sherman

BLOOMSBURY ACADEMIC
NEW YORK • LONDON • OXFORD • NEW DELHI • SYDNEY

BLOOMSBURY ACADEMIC
Bloomsbury Publishing Inc, 1359 Broadway, New York, NY 10018, USA
Bloomsbury Publishing Plc, 50 Bedford Square, London, WC1B 3DP, UK
Bloomsbury Publishing Ireland, 29 Earlsfort Terrace, Dublin 2, D02 AY28, Ireland

BLOOMSBURY, BLOOMSBURY ACADEMIC and the Diana logo are
trademarks of Bloomsbury Publishing Plc

First published in the United States of America 2025

Copyright © Armand Pires and Ryan Sherman, 2025

AASA Logo © The School Superintendents Association (AASA)
Cover images: © istock/Oleksandr Kyrylov

All rights reserved. No part of this publication may be: i) reproduced or transmitted in any form, electronic or mechanical, including photocopying, recording or by means of any information storage or retrieval system without prior permission in writing from the publishers; or ii) used or reproduced in any way for the training, development or operation of artificial intelligence (AI) technologies, including generative AI technologies. The rights holders expressly reserve this publication from the text and data mining exception as per Article 4(3) of the Digital Single Market Directive (EU) 2019/790.

Bloomsbury Publishing Inc does not have any control over, or responsibility for, any third-party websites referred to or in this book. All internet addresses given in this book were correct at the time of going to press. The author and publisher regret any inconvenience caused if addresses have changed or sites have ceased to exist, but can accept no responsibility for any such changes.

A catalog record for this book is available from the Library of Congress

ISBN: HB: 978-1-4758-7504-1
PB: 978-1-4758-7505-8
ePDF: 979-8-7651-5423-6
eBook: 978-1-4758-7506-5

Typeset by Deanta Global Publishing Services, Chennai, India
Printed and bound in the United States of America

For product safety related questions contact productsafety@bloomsbury.com.

To find out more about our authors and books visit www.bloomsbury.com and sign up for our newsletters.

This book would not have been written without those close to the authors, and we'd like to acknowledge their tremendous support.

To Jessica: Thank you for being an amazing wife and mother. Your partnership in life allows me to dream big, think deeply, and follow my passions. I can't begin to thank you enough for your love and support.

To Ella and Grant: Thank you for bringing joy and inspiration to my daily life and work. You motivate me each day to be a better father and remind me of the tremendous value there is in supporting child mental well-being.

To Mom, Dad, Kacie, and Erin: Thank you for modeling careers in the helping professions and for raising me with the belief that student mental health care and education must co-exist in schools. Your belief and support of me during every stage of my life have been a true gift.

—Ryan Sherman

* * *

To my incredible wife, April, whose love, strength, and unwavering support inspire me every day. You challenge me to be a better person and motivate me to contribute to a kinder, more compassionate world.

To my amazing children, Armando and Olivia, whose intelligence, humor, and passion continue to inspire me. I am deeply proud of the remarkable individuals you've become.

To my parents, whose generosity of spirit and persistence shaped who I am; to my siblings, whose enthusiastic support is a constant source of joy; and to my friends and colleagues—your unwavering encouragement propels me forward with gratitude and determination. —Armand Pires

Contents

Acknowledgment viii

1 Introducing a New Approach to an Escalating Problem 1

Part I Defining the Challenge

2 Unraveling the Crisis: The Rise of Youth Mental Health Challenges 9

3 The Limitations of the Pediatric Mental Health System 27

4 The Impact of the Youth Mental Health Crisis on Schools 37

Part II An Expanded Planning Framework

5 The MTSS Framework and Tier 4 47

6 What is MTSS Tier 4, and Why Do Schools Need It? 57

7 Advantages of the Tier 4 Model 69

Part III Putting the Plan into Action

8 Planning for Success 79

9 SEL Tier 4 Components 91

10 Planning for Financial Sustainability 123

11 MTSS Tier 4 Model Examples 135

12 A Call to Action 147

Community Partner Spotlight Resources 153
Notes 155
About the Authors 164

Acknowledgment

This book is written to inspire district leaders to take ownership of student mental health treatment and to provide them with a blueprint for an effective treatment model. However, we'd like to acknowledge the school clinicians, counselors, nurses, teachers, and building leaders who turn treatment models into life-changing interventions for students, especially those in the Medway Public Schools who, through their dedication and hard work, inspire us every day.

1 Introducing a New Approach to an Escalating Problem

If you are reading this book, it is likely because you are deeply concerned about the rapidly growing mental health crisis among school-aged children. Many in education began to sound the alarm around their rapidly increasing concern about student mental health issues, and then Covid-19 happened. With the impact of the Covid-19 pandemic, we have seen a further acceleration in the number of students presenting with mental health issues. In addition to the steep rise in prevalence, we have also seen a marked increase in the intensity of student mental health issues for all groups of school-aged children.

We are at a critical inflection point in schools. While we have waited patiently for social service agencies to spring into action and increase their support, we have seen systems that are overwhelmed. Many of us are frustrated by a system that cannot meet the needs of this growing population of students with needs.

We have seen broadening complexity in navigating the mental health care system on behalf of our students and families. We have also seen extended wait times for treatment for those most in need of intervention. With the system focused on the most urgent cases, often lower-level needs are not being met, which results in an elevation of need. This perpetuates a cycle of being in a critically responsive state without the time or ability to put into practice support to help stem the overwhelming tide of student mental health concerns.

We have continued to cling to a three-tiered, Multi-Tiered System of Support (MTSS) framework as the best approach to meet students' needs. In this approach, hypothetically, a small percentage of students are at the top of the pyramid, with the most critical needs. With the expansion of the number of students in crisis—and their increased intensity—this model, which was developed during more typical times, is inadequate and under-responsive.

Most schools have focused their resources on those students who are in crisis, thereby leaving many students under-supported and under-served. In short, the current system is failing our students.

So what are we going to do about it? How can we, as distinct school leaders, take steps to mitigate this crisis? How can we take active steps necessary to meet the unmet need? How can we rally support and resources to make an impactful change? How can we take control of our circumstances and provide students with what they need?

We believe that this book will offer some answers to those questions. This book is written to provide a practical start to planning support to help mitigate this complicated and multifaceted problem. Within this book, we seek to provide you with a roadmap to plan, build, execute, and fund an approach to increase student mental health issues more effectively. We also offer an expanded organizing framework by taking the well-known Multi-Tiered Systems of Supports model and enhancing it to provide more clarity on possible approaches to this challenge.

The book is organized to take you through the process of developing a comprehensive program to support student mental health needs. Here, you will find a summary of each of the chapters.

Part I: Defining the Challenge

Chapter 2: Unraveling the Crisis: The Rise of Youth Mental Health Challenges

In this chapter, we begin with the good news. We provide data that shows that the risky behavior of children has been on the decline. In many areas, this is great news as behaviors associated with dramatic and significant health outcomes have continued to shrink.

We also provide updated data and statistics to support the focused need to do work in this area. This data is provided both to clarify the critical imperative of the current crisis and to call you to action. It will also provide you with some ideas about the data that can be reviewed, understood, and gathered to support their strategic movement into this area and improve support for students' mental health needs.

Chapter 3: The Limitations of the Pediatric Mental Health System

This chapter reviews the current state of the pediatric mental health system. We review the parameters that have made it more difficult to meet the needs of all students. A review of the current state of the system includes the use of a traditional medical model versus a prevention model, the complexities of the insurance reimbursement system, and the bottlenecks that prevent access for many students, except those from families with the most significant cultural assets.

Chapter 4: The Impact of the Youth Mental Health Crisis in Schools

The continuing student mental health crisis has had significant impacts on schools. This chapter reviews the impact on schools and some of the challenges schools face in working toward solutions.

The unmet needs of students have deeply impacted schools. Unmet student mental health needs directly impact students' ability to find success within schools. From increased absenteeism, behavioral dysregulation, and disengagement, leaders around the country have identified their obligation to meet the needs of all students.

Finally, this chapter outlines the student mental health imperative and our responsibility, as school leaders, to enter this space to find meaningful and sustainable solutions.

Part II: An Expanded Planning Framework

Chapter 5: The MTSS Framework and Tier 4

In this chapter, we conduct a review of the Multi-Tiered Systems of Support model. This well-known model has served as a planning framework to support student learning in the areas of academic achievement and social-emotional learning. This overview explains each of the traditionally situated three tiers.

Importantly, this chapter also provides some reflections on using the current three-tier framework. As part of that reflection, the model's limitations are discussed, including challenges in implementing the three tiers and the gaps in the model. Real-world examples of limitations are also identified. The concept of adding a fourth tier to the traditional MTSS model is also introduced.

Chapter 6: What Is MTSS Tier 4, and Why Do Schools Need It?

Introduced in Chapter 5, the addition of Tier 4 to the traditional MTSS model is discussed. A rationale to support the addition of Tier 4 is provided, including our collective responsibility to move to providing treatment options for students.

In addition, specifics about designing Tier 4 interventions, including some examples of these interventions, are provided. The integration of Tier 4 with the traditional three-tier MTSS model is also discussed.

Chapter 7: Advantages of the Tier 4 Model

This chapter further articulates the advantages of an additional Tier 4 to the traditional MTSS model. You will gain an understanding of how the Tier 4 model helps to improve upon the traditional MTSS approach and pediatric outpatient service models. You will also imagine how a Tier 4 model can better address specific student needs.

Schools nationwide are constantly seeking to better support students with diverse learning profiles and specific mental health concerns. This chapter will examine how a Tier 4 approach can flexibly address precise student learning needs and the most prevalent student mental health concerns. These include school avoidance, disengaged parents/guardians, and student depression and suicidality.

Part III: Putting the Plan into Action

Chapter 8: Planning for Success

This chapter will propel you into action. With an understanding of the enhanced MTSS model, you can begin developing an action plan to support improvement in your context. Within this chapter, you will create a comprehensive plan by following three action steps.

A successful Tier 4 model should be built on an effective planning strategy that includes four critical actions: conducting an environmental scan and needs assessment, developing a communication strategy, and building support and momentum. By the time you finish Chapter 8, you will have the building blocks to develop a plan, integrating an MTSS Tier 4 level to improve the support of your students.

Chapter 9: SEL Tier 4 Components

Chapter 9 focuses on building a Tier 4 model. We'll dive deeper into the four components of a Tier 4 model, which include universal screening, care coordination, in-school outpatient therapy, and wraparound services. Each of these components is explored in detail so that you can determine how to best integrate these types of services into your district's mental health programming.

Chapter 10: Planning for Financial Sustainability

A plan of action is only as good as your ability to implement and fund it. With programs to provide mental health support for students, planning must include how you will fund the plan and continue the supports you have implemented. This chapter provides an approach to consider during plan development to ensure your plan is sustainable. In addition, possible funding sources and partnership opportunities are also included.

Chapter 11: MTSS Tier 4 Model Examples

By this time in the book, you'll understand why you need to upgrade to a Tier 4 model, how to build a Tier 4 model, and how to fund this model. However, even with this high level of understanding, it can sometimes be challenging to envision the end product without an exemplar. In Chapter 11, we'll provide several examples of Tier 4 models so that you can better envision your entry point to creating a Tier 4 model and what a fully integrated model looks like in action. Planning with the end in mind is a time-tested strategy, and this chapter will help you do just that.

Chapter 12: A Call to Action

With an understanding of your Tier 4 model and a plan on how to implement it, you now need to put this plan into action. So, where should you start? We'll probably need to get into the weeds to create the planning documents and templates to make your plan actionable. But who has the time for this? In this chapter, we'll provide you with the planning templates you need to assess your current practice and execute a plan to build a Tier 4 model. But, if even the idea of following a planning template makes you nauseous, then we will also share with you how you can get in touch with us so that we can help your district with this heavy lifting.

Now that you know what is in front of you, we encourage you to read with curiosity and intention. This book will challenge you to examine long-standing approaches and systems within schools, which might feel uncomfortable, and this is okay. With this in mind, our book is designed to help you push past that uncomfortable feeling to take action better to support your student's mental health and academic needs in a new and more effective approach.

Part I
Defining the Challenge

2 Unraveling the Crisis
The Rise of Youth Mental Health Challenges

Now that you have an understanding of why schools must evolve to meet the mental health needs of students, we're going to take a deep dive into the youth mental health crisis in the United States. In this chapter, we'll examine the rise in the prevalence of youth mental health disorders, what role the Covid-19 pandemic played in this rise, and how environmental factors are working against youth's mental well-being. However, before we take a collective look at the US youth, let's zoom into a day in the life of Ella. Ella is a typical sixteen-year-old girl living in New England.

> **Ella's Journal Entry**
> October 6
> Oh, what a day it's been! I'm absolutely exhausted, but I just had to sit down and jot down everything that happened today.
> This morning started way too early. I swear, it felt like I blinked, and my alarm clock was buzzing at 6:30 a.m. Ugh! Mornings are always a struggle for me. I hit snooze a couple of times before finally dragging myself out of bed. A quick shower, and I was out the door in a hurry. Breakfast was just a granola bar—no time for anything more.
> School was, well, school. I had a ton of assignments due today, and I was scrambling to finish them during every free moment I had between classes. Mrs. Johnson's history test felt like a nightmare. I'll need to study harder next time.
> Lunch was a blur, as always. Sat with my usual group of friends, and we chatted about the usual stuff—school drama, weekend plans, and the latest TikTok trends. I also sneaked in a quick scroll through Instagram to see what everyone was up to. After school, it was straight to the soccer field for practice. It's my favorite part of the day. We had a scrimmage today, and I managed to score a goal, which totally boosted my mood. Then, I realized I'd left my phone in my locker, and the anxiety of being disconnected for a couple of hours hit me. Ridiculous, right?

> Back home, I had to rush through my math homework. Seriously, quadratic equations are the bane of my existence. In between problems, I couldn't resist checking my phone. Instagram, TikTok, Snapchat—all the usual suspects. I had to respond to some group chat messages, and then I fell down a rabbit hole of funny cat videos on YouTube. Oops! Dinner was a bit of a blur, too. Mom made spaghetti, and we talked briefly about our days but spent most of the time both looking at our phones. I finally got some time to fully catch up on my messages and post a pic from practice on Instagram once Mom left the table to respond to emails.
>
> As the evening wore on, I tried to get a handle on my homework, but I was so tired. I kept zoning out and had to reread the same paragraph in my English book about a million times. Social media kept calling my name. Just a few more minutes turned into an hour, and suddenly, it was way too late. I'm paying for it now. It's past midnight, and I'm writing this in the dark with my phone's screen turned all the way down so I don't wake up my parents. I know I need more sleep, but there's always something that keeps me up late—schoolwork, friends, or just mindlessly scrolling. Anyway, time to put the phone away and try to get some rest.

Ella's journal entry represented a typical day in the life of an American teenager. Their days are primarily spent in structured activities led by adults, with only 17 percent of school-aged children's time spent in non-structured social or leisure activities.[1] When they have free time, it is often spent making sure they meet academic demands or interacting with peers and adults who are often distracted by their phones. This life structure has helped to make America's youth, for the most part, very safe and physically healthy. However, these new generational norms have also had a very detrimental effect on youth's mental health. In this chapter, we'll explore the environmental factors that have given rise to the youth mental health crisis.

The Good News First

There is no denying that today's youth are grappling with mental health concerns at an unprecedented prevalence. The rise in mental health issues coincides with several macro developments, such as access to social media, a lack of unstructured free time, and increased academic demands. While these changes have adversely impacted youth mental health, some benefits have emerged from these macro shifts.

The Benefits of Socializing Online

American youth generally engage in fewer risky behaviors than previous generations. This risk-averse behavior has led to a decline in the prevalence of teenage drinking, smoking, and pregnancies. Most of us agree that these changes are positive, and it can be hypothesized that they result from the shifting dynamics of how teenagers socially engage, primarily through the use of their phones.

One of the primary reasons iGen youth are less likely to engage in risky behaviors is the prevalence of smartphones and the digital world. They spend significant time online, whether on social media, playing video games, or using various apps. In fact, nearly all teens had access to a smartphone as of 2022; this is up from 73 percent, see Figure 2.1, in 2014–15.[2] This constant connectivity provides them with an enhanced level of physical safety, alternative forms of entertainment, and social interaction, reducing the appeal of traditional risky behaviors.

In addition to having access to a smartphone, most teens spend much more time on social media. According to recent data, 48 percent of adolescents

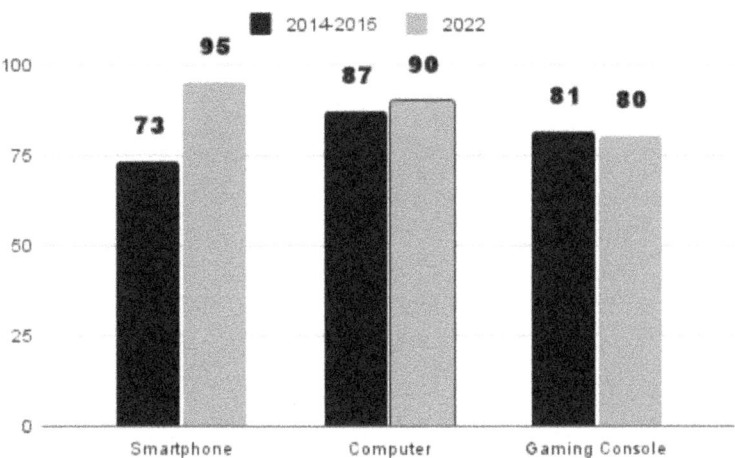

Figure 2.1 Percentage of US teens who say they have access to the mentioned devices. Pew Research Center: https://www.pewresearch.org/internet/fact-sheet/teens-and-internet-device-access-fact

spend a mean of five hours per day on social media, and 12 percent spend more than ten hours per day on social media.[3] This is a remarkable increase from 2013 when teens spent an average of one and a half hours per day on social media.[4] Naturally, this shows a shift in how teens are interacting with each other. Teen drinking, smoking, and pregnancies have long been associated with risky behaviors that occur during in-person social settings. With teen social interactions moving away from unstructured in-person interactions, the prevalence of these risky behaviors has declined. These changes in behavior can also be connected to the evolution of the American teen-parent relationship.

Helicopter Parenting Has Its Perks

Helicopter parenting is defined as parents who are so obsessed with their kid's every move that they would attach a propeller to their beanie if it meant they could hover more closely. While this definition feels accurate, a more formal definition characterizes helicopter parenting as a style marked by excessive overinvolvement and attention to a child's every activity, often being overly controlling and protective. No matter how you define it, helicopter parenting is often associated with a negative connotation due to its link to a lack of developing a child's independence and an inability to develop problem-solving skills. However, when it comes to adolescents engaging in risky behaviors, helicopter parenting does provide some benefits.

A lack of youth development fostered by overly involved and controlling parents has led to a delay in adolescent independence. For example, youth are reaching traditional markers of independence, such as obtaining a driver's license or leaving home for college or work, later in life than previous generations. These life milestones traditionally lead to teens having more freedom and autonomy. Without these freedoms, adolescents are less likely to engage in behaviors like illicit substance use, Figure 2.2, and are less likely to be sexually active, Figure 2.3. In addition to influencing the delay of adolescent freedoms, helicopter parents have also had an impact on teen priorities.

Parents of today's youth tend to be more involved in their children's lives, including monitoring their activities and discouraging risky behaviors. This heightened parental involvement can act as a protective factor, reducing teen substance use and sexual activity. This type of parental involvement

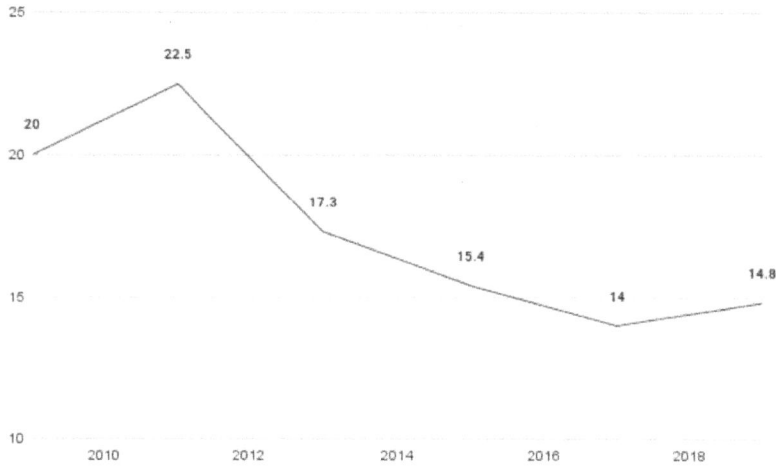

Figure 2.2 Percentage of high school students who ever used illicit drugs. CDC Youth Risk Behavior Survey

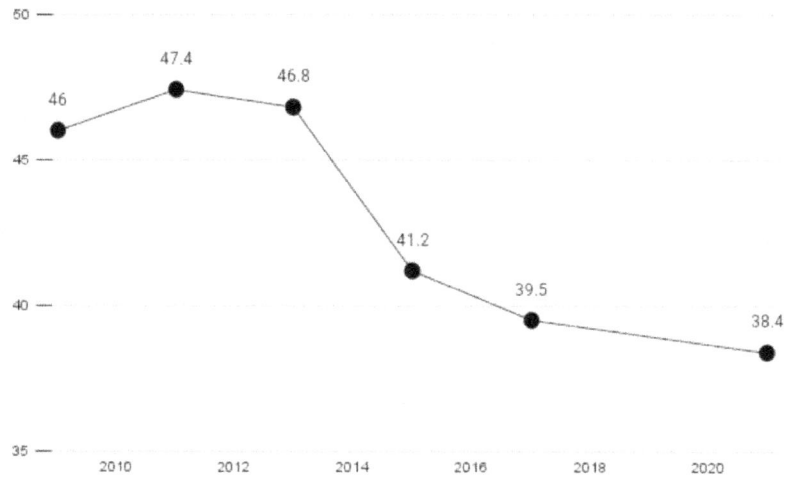

Figure 2.3 Percentage of high school students who ever had sex. CDC Youth Risk Behavior Survey: https://www.cdc.gov/healthyyouth/data/yrbs/pdf/yrbs_data-summary-trends_report2023_508.pdf

may also be affecting adolescents' priorities as youth today place greater emphasis on academic achievement, extracurricular activities, and building their online identities. These pursuits can take up much of their time and attention, leaving less room for risky behaviors. While a shift in parental involvement and social interactions for youth has led to a decrease in risky youth behaviors, it has also had a devastating effect on adolescents' mental health.

The Youth Mental Health Crisis in America

The youth mental health crisis in the United States is a complex and multifaceted issue characterized by a significant increase in the prevalence of mental health challenges among young people, ranging from children to adolescents and young adults. Over the past two decades, this crisis has raised growing concerns and demands for urgent attention.

At its core, the youth mental health crisis is marked by a surge in the incidence of mental health disorders among young individuals. Conditions like depression, anxiety, bipolar disorder, eating disorders, and attention deficit hyperactivity disorder (ADHD) have become increasingly common. These conditions can profoundly affect a young person's emotional well-being, cognitive functioning, social interactions, and overall quality of life.

One of the critical aspects of this crisis is the age of onset. Mental health disorders are often identified during childhood or adolescence, making early intervention critical. When left unaddressed, these issues can persist into adulthood, potentially leading to chronic mental health challenges that have a lasting impact on a person's life. Before exploring the factors contributing to the youth mental health crisis, it is vital to understand how the prevalence of youth mental health disorders has surged over the past decades.

The Pre-Pandemic Rise in Prevalence

Often, the Covid-19 pandemic is viewed as the starting point for the youth mental health crisis. However, the rise in youth mental health needs started over a decade ago. Between 2011 and 2015, youth psychiatry visits to emergency departments for depression, anxiety, and behavioral challenges increased by 28 percent.[5] Additionally, between 2007 and 2018, suicide rates among youth from ages ten to twenty-four increased by 57 percent.[6] These staggering changes look even more dire when you examine high school mental health data over the same time frame.

From 2009–19, most indicators of youth mental health and suicide trended upward. Over this period, more teens experienced feelings of sadness or

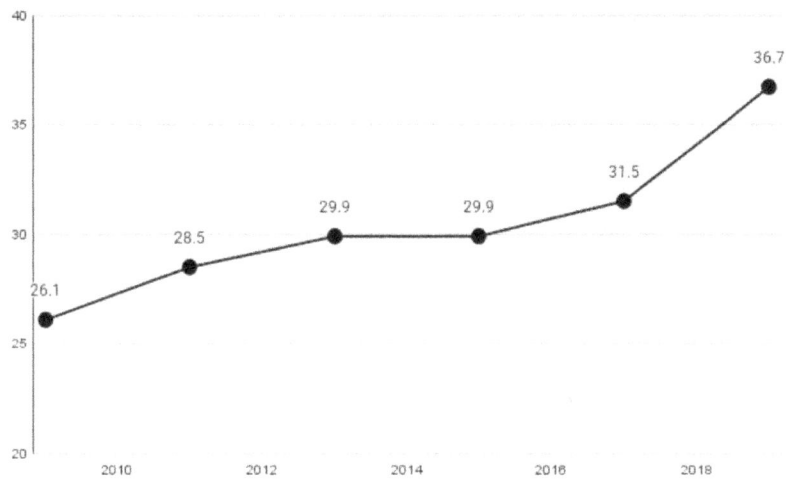

Figure 2.4 Percentage of high school students who experienced feelings of sadness or hopelessness. CDC Youth Risk Behavior Survey: https://www.cdc.gov/healthyyouth/data/yrbs/pdf/yrbs_data-summary-trends_report2023_508.pdf

hopelessness, regardless of race/ethnicity, and astonishingly, nearly 50 percent of females reported persistent feelings of sadness or hopelessness (see Figure 2.4).

Additionally, during the decade leading up to the pandemic, about one in five teens seriously considered suicide, and the number of teens who made a suicide plan rose over this time. Teen suicide attempts increased by over 40 percent during these ten years, with female teens more likely to attempt suicide than male teens, Figure 2.5.

The prevalence of youth mental health concerns was already approaching crisis levels by 2019. Unfortunately, the Covid-19 pandemic proved to be the breaking point that set the prevalence of youth mental health concerns skyrocketing.

The Post-Pandemic Youth Mental Health Crisis

With the prevalence of youth mental health concerns on the rise for a decade, it didn't appear that the situation could get much worse, and then the Covid-19 pandemic hit. The pandemic added a new layer of urgency to the youth mental health crisis. The disruptions caused by the pandemic led to mental health risk factors such as lost connections with trusted adults due to school closures, social isolation, and heightened uncertainty.

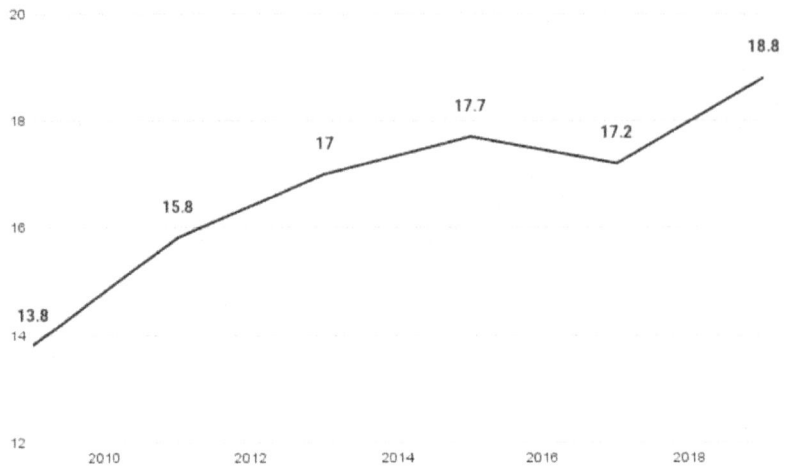

Figure 2.5 Percentage of high school students who seriously considered attempting suicide. CDC Youth Risk Behavior Survey: https://www.cdc.gov/healthyyouth/data/yrbs/pdf/yrbs_data-summary-trends_report2023_508.pdf

The pandemic also caused some children to lose access to food, housing, mental health care, and social services. Children may have also suffered from Covid-19 themselves or lost a loved one due to the disease. These pandemic-generated factors exacerbated stress, anxiety, feelings of sadness and hopelessness, isolation, and suicidality among young individuals, intensifying the need for mental health support.

Research conducted in 2021 that covered 80,000 youth from around the world found that depressive and anxiety symptoms doubled during the pandemic.[7] Similar trends are evident when looking at emergency room data, which showed that suspected suicide attempts were over 50 percent for adolescent girls in the United States in 2021.[8] A survey conducted by the Centers for Disease Control (CDC) across high schools in the United States confirms this rapid increase in teen mental health concerns.

In 2021, according to the CDC, nearly a third of high school students in the United States shared that they have experienced poor mental health in the last thirty days. This feeling of poor mental health was evident when looking at teens who experienced persistent feelings of sadness or hopelessness, 42 percent, and those who seriously considered attempting suicide, 22 percent. These represent a 14 percent increase in teens who had feelings of sadness

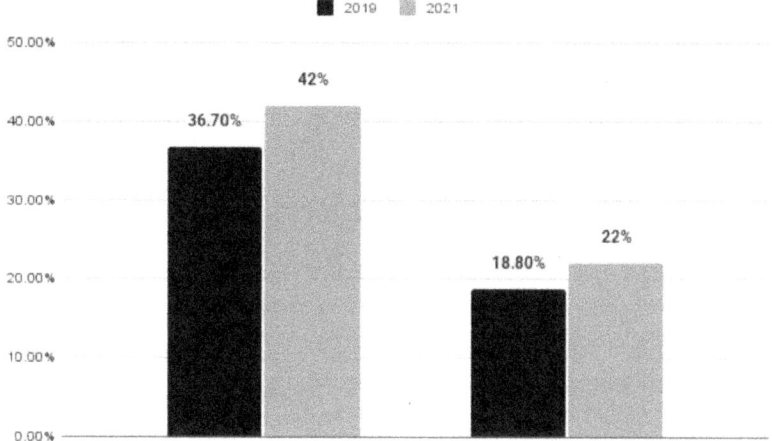

Figure 2.6 Pre- and post-pandemic high school student mental health. CDC Youth Risk Behavior Survey: https://www.cdc.gov/healthyyouth/data/yrbs/pdf/yrbs_data-summary-trends_report2023_508.pdf

or hopelessness and a 16 percent increase in teens who seriously considered attempting suicide since 2019, Figure 2.6.

Thankfully, the Covid-19 pandemic is behind us. However, remnants of harmful environmental factors remain that will likely continue to give rise to youth mental health concerns. Some of these elements were present before the pandemic and have persisted. Others were born due to the pandemic but are likely to remain current in children's lives for the foreseeable future.

A Product of Their Environment: What's Fueling the Mental Health Crisis

Although we are still likely years away from researchers truly understanding what factors are at the source of the adolescent mental health crisis in the United States, several front-running environmental factors that could be at the root of the problem have emerged in recent years. These well-researched hypotheses include the growing use of digital media, increased screen time, and the changing dynamics of social and home life for children and adolescents.[9,10,11,12,13] Each of these elements likely has played a part in inciting the youth mental health crisis. Still, due to its impact on students' social and sleep habits, the rise of digital media is often cited as enemy number one.

Digital Media and Youth Mental Health

The rise of social media and digital technology has transformed how young people interact and communicate. While technology has many benefits, it has also introduced new challenges, including pressure to curate a perfect online image, fear of missing out, and sleep interruptions, which can contribute to feelings of inadequacy and loneliness. These challenges have led to a glaring correlation between the amount of time youth are spending on social media and mental health concerns.[14]

Youth Social Media Use and Mental Health Concerns

Youth social media use in the United States is practically universal. Up to 95 percent of adolescents ages thirteen to seventeen use at least one social media platform, and more than a third of youth share that they use social media "almost constantly."[15] Although social media use is often associated with teens, just under 40 percent of children ages eight to twelve also use social media.[16] This widespread use has allowed for the mental health harms associated with social media to potentially impact most youth in the United States.

A longitudinal study of over 6,500 US teens found that adolescents who spent more than three hours per day on social media faced double the risk of experiencing poor mental health outcomes, which included symptoms of anxiety and depression.[17] As of 2021, students in grades 8 and 10 were found to spend an average of three and a half hours per day on social media.[18] Studies of this age group have found that in addition to an increased risk of experiencing poor mental health, social media use is predictive of a subsequent decrease in life satisfaction.[19]

In contrast, studies that have limited social media use for young adults improved subject life satisfaction, anxiety, depression, and happiness by 25–40 percent.[20] This improvement is similar to self-help and group and individual therapy interventions.[21] Although it is clear that average social media use by youth is detrimental to their mental health, the causes of what is driving this correlation are murky. Some hypotheses include youth needing to "perfect" their online image or the constant fear of missing out.

Perfecting Your Online Image

The quest for perfection on social media platforms has become a pervasive aspect of teenage culture, with adolescents often feeling pressured to meticulously curate and maintain an idealized online image. This desire for perfection can have profound implications for their mental health. Adolescents may find themselves trapped in a cycle of comparison, constantly measuring their worth against the seemingly flawless lives depicted by their peers. The unrealistic standards perpetuated by social media can contribute to feelings of inadequacy, fostering a sense of discontent and self-doubt. This perpetual pursuit of an ideal image may lead to increased stress, anxiety, and even depression among teenagers as they grapple with the discrepancy between their online persona and the complexities of their natural lives.[21]

Furthermore, the relentless pursuit of a perfect online image can lead to a disconnect from authentic self-expression. Teens may feel compelled to conform to popular trends and societal expectations, sacrificing their individuality in the process. The pressure to conform to narrow beauty standards or conformist ideals may stifle creativity and personal growth. In an era dominated by the constant documentation of life events on social media, the focus on external validation can overshadow the importance of developing a strong sense of self. This pursuit of the perfect online persona, when combined with the fear of missing out, can lead to negative experiences when it comes to social media use and youths' mental health.

The Fear of Missing Out (FOMO)

The Fear of Missing Out (FOMO) phenomenon has become increasingly prevalent in the lives of teenagers, mainly driven by the pervasive nature of social media. The constant exposure to their peers' seemingly exciting and glamorous activities can instill a profound fear of being excluded from social experiences. As teenagers scroll through carefully curated timelines showcasing the highlights of others' lives, a sense of inadequacy and anxiety may take root. The fear of missing out on rewarding social interactions or exciting events can contribute to heightened stress levels and negatively impact their mental well-being.[22]

Moreover, the continuous comparison facilitated by social media intensifies the FOMO experience. Adolescents may find themselves constantly measuring their own lives against the perceived vibrancy of their peers' social circles. This perpetual state of comparison can lead to feelings of isolation and a distorted sense of self-worth. The fear of missing out can escalate into self-imposed pressure to engage in social activities simply to maintain an online presence, potentially leading to burnout and a compromised mental state. Of course, the more time they spend on social media, the greater the sense of FOMO youth often experience. Likewise, social media use, especially in the evening, can cause sleep disruptions that only perpetuate youth mental health concerns.

Mobile Devices and Sleep

Sleep deprivation is often categorized as a public health crisis that is under-reported, with significant negative physical and mental health implications. For our youth, sleep is crucial, balancing cognitive, physical, social, and emotional development. However, we know that many of our young people are sleep-deprived. In fact, 57.8 percent of middle and 72.7 percent of high school students report not getting enough sleep on school nights.[23] Adequate sleep is not merely a physiological necessity; it serves as a cornerstone for psychological resilience and coping with academic and personal challenges. Although many factors can contribute to youth sleep deprivation, digital media use, particularly at night, can lead to sleep disturbances that negatively affect youth mental health.

As technology continues to permeate every facet of modern life, the impact of screen use on sleep patterns has become a pertinent concern in the context of student mental health. Screens, whether in the form of smartphones, tablets, or computers, emit blue light that suppresses melatonin production, a hormone crucial for regulating sleep-wake cycles. The prevalence of this sleep cycle is pervasive among youth, with 69 percent of teens taking their mobile devices to bed and nearly one in three adolescents reporting using screen media until midnight or later.[24] The ubiquity of screens in educational and social environments has led to increased exposure, disrupting circadian rhythms and compromising students' sleep quality and duration. In addition to the known association between evening screen time and sleep disruptions, recent studies have shown a consistent relationship between social media use and poor sleep quality.

A systematic review of over forty studies found a positive correlation between excessive social media use and reduced sleep duration, sleep difficulties, and depression among youth.[25] Poor sleep, often caused by excessive social media and screen use, has been linked to disrupted adolescent brain development, depressive symptoms, and suicidal thoughts and behaviors.[26,27] When considering evening device use, many people will wonder about the parent/guardian's role in helping adolescents who aren't capable of self-regulating device use, putting guardrails in place. Interestingly enough, adult behavior within the home is likely to have a negative impact on youth sleep, device use, and, consequently, their mental health.

The Assault on Family Protective Factors

Parents and guardians are pivotal in contributing to protective factors associated with youth mental health. A secure and supportive family environment, characterized by open communication, emotional warmth, and positive parent-child relationships, serves as a fundamental protective factor. Involved parenting, where parents actively engage in their child's life, provides a sense of stability and belonging, fostering resilience in the face of stressors.

Additionally, parents can contribute to their child's mental well-being by promoting effective coping strategies, instilling a positive self-image, and encouraging the development of strong interpersonal skills. By being attentive to their child's emotional needs, modeling healthy behaviors, and offering guidance, parents significantly influence the protective factors that contribute to their youth's mental health and overall well-being.[28] Unfortunately, modern family environments and parent behaviors often conflict with the promotion of protective factors.

The impact of adult behaviors, particularly mobile device use and the rise in remote work, can be detrimental to the well-being of children. In contemporary society, the prevalence of mobile device usage among parents has significantly increased. Similarly, post-pandemic working conditions have allowed for more parents to work from home, which on the surface seems to be supportive of child raising but may also be negatively impacting the mental health of youth. Together, as parents immerse themselves in digital distractions and home working conditions, a critical consequence emerges—a lack of attention and engagement with their children.

Excessive use of mobile devices among parents poses a formidable barrier to meaningful connections with their children, consequently shaping the emotional well-being and sense of importance experienced by young minds. As parents immerse themselves in digital distractions, the time and attention traditionally devoted to familial interactions diminish.[29] Children seeking validation and emotional engagement from their caregivers find themselves competing with screens for parental attention. The visual and emotional cues crucial for bonding are often lost in the glow of devices, creating a disconnect that extends beyond the immediate moment.

A lack of genuine connection can foster feelings of neglect and emotional distance in children, adversely impacting their self-esteem and overall emotional well-being.[29] The sense of importance children derive from interactions with their parents is compromised, as they may perceive themselves as secondary to the allure of screens. Thus, the pervasive nature of excessive screen time becomes a significant contributor to the evolving dynamics within familial relationships, influencing the emotional landscape and the prevalence of mental health concerns of today's youth. The mass shift of parents working from home that occurred after the Covid-19 pandemic is likely having a similar impact on children's mental health.

The shift toward remote work, while offering flexibility, has contributed to a transformation in parental availability. The limited quality time spent together is a significant concern as it compromises the crucial moments for parent-child bonding and emotional connection. Furthermore, the negative consequences extend beyond temporal limitations, encompassing the stressors associated with increased work hours at home.[29] This stress becomes an indirect factor impacting children's mental health, highlighting the intricate relationship between parental work conditions and the psychological well-being of their offspring.

When considering the combined effects of mobile device use and increased remote work, a synergistic impact emerges, intensifying the challenges youth face. The cumulative effect on children's mental health becomes apparent, manifesting in reduced emotional support from distracted parents and heightened feelings of neglect and isolation among the younger demographic. In addition to the changing dynamics at home, youth have also experienced increased academic demands that have been detrimental to their mental well-being.

Academic Demands

The intertwining challenges of standardized testing, extensive homework commitments, and the intense pressure associated with college admissions form a trifecta that significantly impacts the mental health of students in the United States. The prevalence of standardized testing in elementary and middle school settings has become a cause for concern, as the weight placed on assessment outcomes induces stress and anxiety in young learners, influencing their cognitive and emotional development.

Moving into high school, the substantial time dedicated to homework greatly contributes to heightened stress levels and compromised well-being. The pervasive culture of rigorous academic coursework, coupled with extracurricular commitments, poses a substantial burden on students, potentially leading to sleep deprivation and heightened anxiety. Furthermore, the formidable pressure associated with gaining admission to top colleges exacerbates mental health challenges, fostering a competitive atmosphere marked by anxiety, fear of failure, and burnout.

The prevalence of standardized testing in elementary and middle school settings in the United States has emerged as a source of concern due to its discernible negative impact on student's mental health. The consequential weight placed on the outcomes of these assessments instills a sense of pressure and anxiety in young learners, often exacerbating stress levels during formative years of cognitive and emotional development.[30]

The high-stakes nature of these tests, coupled with the potential implications for academic advancement and institutional evaluations, contributes to an environment where students may experience heightened apprehension, fear of failure, and self-doubt. The psychological toll incurred during these early stages can have lasting effects, shaping not only academic performance but also influencing the overall mental well-being of students. In addition to the stress associated with standardized testing, today's youth spend more time on homework, which can negatively impact their mental well-being.[31]

The substantial amount of time devoted to homework among students in the United States may be contributing to the increasing prevalence of mental health concerns. The demanding nature of academic coursework and extracurricular commitments places an onerous burden on students, often leading to heightened stress levels and compromised well-being.[32]

The pervasive culture of extensive homework assignments may result in insufficient time for adequate rest, leisure, and social activities crucial for holistic personal development.[33] The cumulative effect of prolonged periods spent on homework not only impinges upon the mental and emotional equilibrium of students but may also contribute to sleep deprivation and heightened anxiety. Coinciding with increased homework demands is the pressure students face regarding college admissions.

The heightened pressure associated with gaining admission to top colleges among high school students in America constitutes a significant contributor to the negative impact on their mental health. The fiercely competitive nature of the college admissions process, exacerbated by societal expectations and the perceived prestige associated with elite institutions, engenders a pervasive sense of anxiety and fear of failure. Students navigating this intricate journey grapple with the weight of expectations from themselves, their families, and their communities, leading to heightened stress levels and emotional distress.[34] The relentless pursuit of academic excellence and the competitive atmosphere surrounding college admissions may result in various mental health challenges, including burnout and self-doubt.

The introduction of standardized testing, extensive homework commitments, and the intense pressure associated with college admissions constitute a formidable trio that leaves an indelible mark on the mental health of youth in the United States. From the early stages of education to the pivotal years of high school, the persistent weight of these challenges manifests as heightened stress, anxiety, and compromised well-being.

When these academic pressures are considered in the context of youths' constant connection to screens and social media, the absence of protective factors within the home, and a worldwide pandemic, it is easy to account for the dramatic rise in mental health issues over the last ten years. Coupled with the steep increase in youth mental health concerns, schools are dealing with an under-equipped pediatric mental health system, leaving them with no place to turn for support.

Key Takeaways

- Today's youth take part in less risky behavior, such as substance use and sexual intercourse, than previous generations.

- The prevalence of youth mental health disorders has grown significantly over the last ten years.
- The Covid-19 pandemic spurred higher rates of youth mental health concerns and suicidality.
- In addition to the pandemic, the main drivers of increased youth mental health rates are digital media use, a reduction in protective factors within the home, and increased academic demands.

What's Next?

In the next chapter, we'll explore why the pediatric mental health system is broken, how it got here, and why schools should not be waiting for it to improve anytime soon. We'll also explore how the lack of pediatric mental health providers and the limited daily window for school-aged children to be seen by a provider has led to an unprecedented access bottleneck.

3 The Limitations of the Pediatric Mental Health System

"I recommend talking to your student's pediatrician." These are often the first words said by a school counselor when speaking with a parent or guardian about their student's mental health concerns. This advice, on the surface, makes total sense. Pediatricians are some of the most highly trained and knowledgeable health professionals in the healthcare system. Also, they likely have a strong relationship with the child, and very often, the parent or guardian is comfortable seeking their advice. However, when we take a step back from these personal relationships between the child, their family, and their pediatrician and examine the pediatric mental health system as a whole, it's easy to notice several glaring limitations.

As detailed in the previous chapter, the need for pediatric mental health services has exploded in the last decade. However, the pediatric mental health system has failed to meet these needs due to limitations connected to mental health training for pediatricians, insurance reimbursement, and mental health clinician availability. These limitations have created a massive backlog of patients who aren't able to access timely and effective mental health care. In this chapter, we'll explore the underlying causes of these limitations to understand better why schools must adjust their practices to match the pediatric mental health care system's current capabilities. Let's start this examination by diving into how pediatricians are trained in the area of mental health.

Where Have All the Mental Health Providers Gone?

The Plight of the Pediatrician

For the last forty-five years, there has been a recognition that pediatricians are not adequately trained in behavioral and mental health. Over this time, the prevalence of mental health conditions in children and adolescents has increased significantly. However, 65 percent of pediatricians surveyed by the American Academy of Pediatrics indicated that they lacked training in recognizing and treating mental health problems. In fact, 40 percent responded that they lacked the ability to diagnose mental health problems, and more than 50 percent reported they lacked confidence in their ability to treat these patients.[1] With so many children in need of mental health support, why don't pediatricians feel prepared to diagnose and treat their patients? To answer this question, we must dig into the type of training they receive.

It takes eleven strenuous years of education and training to become a pediatrician. This includes a four-year bachelor's degree, four years of medical school, and three years of a medical residency. However, historically, pediatric residency training requirements did not stipulate curricular elements or assessment requirements in behavioral and mental health. The Accreditation Council for Graduate Medical Education has recently mandated block rotations in developmental-behavioral pediatrics. The recommendations include mental health surveillance, screening, recognition, and counseling in the developmental-behavioral pediatrics curriculum.[2] Unfortunately, this increased level of training has yet to make a felt impact.

Attention deficit hyperactivity disorder (ADHD) was the first pediatric mental health condition to have a published set of guidelines and is the condition for which pediatricians receive the most formal training to diagnose and treat. Today, ADHD is screened for more than any other pediatric mental health issue and is the condition for which pediatricians report the most confidence in diagnosis and treatment.[3]

However, training is much less extensive for pediatricians on how to identify and treat mental health conditions like anxiety and depression, whose prevalence, as mentioned in Chapter 2, is growing at a significant rate. This lack of training, to no fault of their own, leaves pediatricians with no other choice but to rely on referring their patients to mental health specialists. This wouldn't necessarily be a bad thing, except that there aren't even close enough of these specialists to go around.

Referring to the Abyss

Pediatricians regularly refer their patients to specialists for various needs, from neurology to orthopedics. With the exception of specific geographical regions of the United States, children are usually able to access timely specialty care. However, access to child psychiatric services is an entirely different story.

The significant and steady rise in child and adolescent mental health challenges has resulted in an increased referral rate to child psychiatric services. Unfortunately, provider growth within this discipline has not expanded at the same rate. The American Academy of Child and Adolescent Psychiatry estimates that 47 child psychiatrists per 100,000 children would be a sufficient number of providers to support the current level of pediatric mental health needs.[4,5] As of now, the United States has 9.75 child psychiatrists per 100,000 children.

Based on these estimates, the country would need approximately 38,000 child and adolescent psychiatrists to meet the current demand. This discrepancy begins to appear much worse when looking at the shortage of psychiatrists by state. Although Massachusetts has a high of 26.5 psychiatrists per 100,000 children, which is still far below the necessary amount, states like Idaho have an alarmingly low ratio of 3.3 child psychiatrists to 100,000 children.[6] This shortage of psychiatrists, Figure 3.1, often leaves children waiting months for appointments.

After a referral is placed by a pediatrician, a child suspected of having mental health conditions can spend months on a waiting list for evaluation from a specialist. In fact, in a National Survey of Healthcare Organizations and

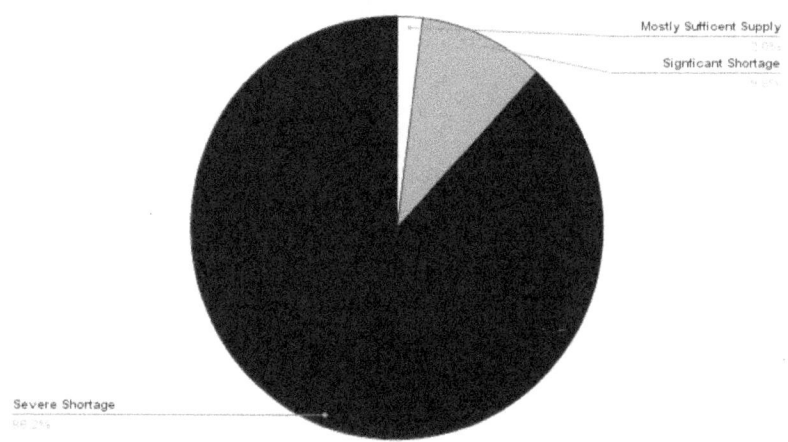

Figure 3.1 Practicing pediatric psychiatrists by 100K per child by State American Academy of Child & Adolescent Psychiatry: https://www.aacap.org/aacap/Advocacy/Federal_and_State_Initiatives/Workforce_Maps/Home.aspx

Systems, more than 85 percent of practices found it difficult to obtain help with evidence-based elements of pediatric mental health care.[7]

This leaves pediatricians in a challenging position. They must go it alone, supporting patients with mental health conditions for which they have not been adequately trained to diagnose and treat, or ask their patients, often in a time of significant need, to wait several months to be seen by a specialist. Talk about being stuck between a rock and a hard place. So, what gave rise to a system that is so broken and puts patients and pediatricians in such undesirable positions? Well, when trying to find the source of most problems, it is often helpful to follow the money.

Show Me the Money... Wait, What Money?

Adding to the lack of training for pediatricians and the absence of available mental health specialists, inadequate reimbursement from government and private insurance plans remains one of the main barriers to mental health care access. Overwhelmed by low reimbursement rates compared with other services and the effort required to appeal, many pediatricians have opted instead to refer out many of their pediatric mental health problems.

However, mental health care providers are reimbursed at the same meager rate, which has led to a shortage of providers and patient waitlists that are often hundreds deep. Although reimbursement rates for pediatric mental health services are low across the board, public health insurance reimbursement rates are minute. For mental health care agencies serving the publicly insured, these tiny reimbursement rates make hiring and retaining staff nearly impossible.

Most publicly insured children are insured through a version of the federal and state joint insurance coverage called Medicaid. Medicaid covers more than 20 percent of all Americans with mental health disorders, and 50 percent of those insured by Medicaid with a severe mental illness report unmet needs.[8] The correlation between unmet mental health needs, the lack of clinicians, and low reimbursement rates can easily be made.

Medicaid reimbursement rates are generally well below Medicare, public insurance for those age sixty-five or older, and are well below commercial rates. In fact, when examining psychiatrist reimbursement rates, it was found that Medicaid paid psychiatrists at 81.0 percent of Medicare rates.[9,10] Looking even deeper, it has been shown that private insurers pay nearly 150 percent of Medicare rates for physician services.[11] So, what is incentivizing pediatric mental health providers to accept public insurance? Well, nothing really, and many pediatric mental health providers have moved away from accepting private insurance as well.

Private insurance certainly reimburses pediatric mental health care providers at a higher rate than public insurance. However, it's not that attractive of a proposition for mental health clinicians to accept private pay insurance. Reimbursement rates for mental health services can vary significantly among private insurers, and private insurance plans often have specific limitations on the types and frequency of covered mental health services.

For example, there may be caps on the number of therapy sessions or exclusions for certain types of therapies. Adding to the burden, obtaining credentials to become an in-network provider for commercial insurers can be lengthy and complex, often requiring detailed documentation and compliance with various standards for each private insurer you plan to submit for reimbursement.

As a mental health provider, you must also correctly code and document your services to bill them. As you can tell, although mental health care providers are reimbursed at higher rates by private insurers, the administrative workload associated with billing is significant. This, along with the overwhelming demand for services, has paved the way for a large number of pediatric mental health providers only to accept patients who can pay out of pocket for their services.

The Covid-19 pandemic helped set the table for pediatric mental health clinicians to dramatically shift how they meet with patients and seek reimbursement. The pandemic created a vast demand for pediatric mental health clinicians and opened the doors to teletherapy, vastly expanding the geographic region they are able to serve. This shift changed the landscape for clinicians, who now have the opportunity to exclusively accept patients who have the ability to pay for their out-of-pocket services.

Out-of-pocket or direct payment is when patients pay providers for their services directly. They allow providers to set their own rates for services, often higher than the reimbursement rates offered by insurance companies. This can lead to an increased revenue per session compared to billing insurance. This payment method essentially eliminates all of the headaches for pediatric mental health providers associated with billing insurance that were described previously in this chapter. Sounds appealing, doesn't it? Of course, it does, which is why many providers have moved to this payment method. However, the unintended consequence of this shift has created a monumental bottleneck for pediatric mental health services, which has led to long wait lists for children to receive the care they need.

The Ultimate Bottleneck

Let's take a moment to reset the pediatric mental health landscape. Pediatricians are not thoroughly trained to diagnose and treat mental health concerns. As a result, they refer to mental health specialists. There is a shortage of pediatric mental health specialists, which creates a backlog of pending referrals and long patient wait lists. Due to a limited supply of providers and a high patient demand, mental health specialists can decide which types of payment methods they accept. Since reimbursement rates are low and administrative hurdles are vast when it comes to accepting public or private health insurance, many providers have opted only to receive direct payments from patients.

As you can see, this system of care does not lend itself to timely diagnosis and treatment for most pediatric patients, especially if you plan to pay through public health insurance. The picture becomes bleaker still when you consider the limited hours in which most children are available to be seen by a mental health provider. To examine this issue, let's consider the case of Grant.

> Grant is in the sixth grade, and he gets in trouble at school a lot. He is quick to get angry, has a hard time sitting still in class, and, when corrected by his teachers, is frequently oppositional. Recently, he got into a fight at recess, and his mother caught him vaping with a friend at home. Suspended from school and unsure what to do, his mother took him to see his pediatrician for advice.
>
> Grant's pediatrician is aware of his behaviors and recently screened him for ADHD. Although Grant has many of the symptoms of a child with ADHD, he does not present with inattention. Unwilling to chalk it up to just "bad behavior" but unsure of whether or not Grant could be suffering from anxiety, he refers him to a child psychiatrist. After an eight-week wait

and another suspension from school, Grant is seen by a psychiatrist who diagnosed him with generalized anxiety disorder.

Grant is then referred to a therapist to gain skills to understand and cope with his feelings. The good news is a therapist is available to see him in two weeks but only accepts out-of-pocket payments. Since Grant's family cannot afford to pay directly, he is placed on a waitlist for patients insured by Medicaid. He waits and waits, and in two months, his family receives a call that an appointment has opened up if he is willing to meet virtually or during the school day.

Due to his challenges with sitting still, his family is leery of Grant getting much out of teletherapy. Additionally, they don't have the ability to miss periods of work each week to bring him to an appointment during school hours. As a result, he waits another two months before gaining access to a therapist who accepts Medicaid, will meet with him in person, and has after-school or weekend availability. In total, eight months have passed between when Grant was referred by his pediatrician to a mental health specialist and when he had his first appointment with a therapist.

When considering Grant's case, his issues with obtaining timely care were largely due to the shortage of child psychiatrists, the fact that he holds public health insurance, and his family's preference for in-person therapy, but the delay in care was also due to the scheduling bottleneck that exists when trying to schedule pediatric mental health appointments during after-school hours or on the weekends.

The Search for Pediatric Mental Health Appointments

Imagine you were one of the people trying to buy a ticket for the Taylor Swift Eras Tour. You, along with millions of other fans, flocked to Ticketmaster's website simultaneously, leading to an unprecedented surge in traffic. The website's infrastructure was not equipped to handle such a massive volume of users simultaneously. This caused the website to slow down significantly and crash several times; users encountered numerous error messages and experienced timeouts, and soon-to-be purchasers got kicked out of the queue and had to start over.

Those who managed to get into the queue faced extremely long wait times. The system's inability to process the high volume of requests quickly led to a bottleneck, where the demand far exceeded the website's capacity to handle transactions efficiently, and worst of all, due to the high demand, the website could not update its inventory. So, many fans found that by the time they reached the purchasing stage, the tickets they wanted were no longer available.

This bottleneck highlighted significant weaknesses in Ticketmaster's infrastructure and led to widespread criticism from fans and the media. It also prompted discussions about the need for better ticket sales systems and fairer distribution methods to manage high-demand events. Although gaining far less media attention, this same type of scenario is playing out each day as the majority of school-aged children in need of mental health support are seeking care from a limited pool of clinicians during after-school hours or on weekends. As a result, there just simply aren't enough provider hours to go around in this limited window to meet the demand.

The shortage of mental health pediatric providers and the scheduling limitations surrounding appointments for children have a trickle-down effect on school systems. The impact of the youth mental health crisis overwhelming the pediatric mental health system has created a need for schools to provide mental health support at an unprecedented level. In the next chapter, you'll explore how this shift in student needs is impacting school systems and district leaders.

Key Takeaways

- Pediatricians receive inadequate training on how to identify and treat mental health concerns.
- There is a national shortage of pediatric mental health providers.
- Reimbursement rates for providers to treat child mental health concerns are underwhelmingly low for both public and private health insurance.
- Providers are incentivized to exclusively accept out-of-pocket payments from patients due to low insurance reimbursement rates.

- Most children are able to be seen by a therapist only during after-school hours or on the weekends.
- The lack of pediatrician training, the national shortage of pediatric mental health providers, low reimbursement rates for pediatric mental health services, and a limited window for children to be seen by a therapist have resulted in an ineffective pediatric mental health system with extremely long waits for patients to access the care they need.

What's Next?

The next chapter dives into the impact that the youth mental health crisis is having on schools. We'll examine how student mental health has quickly become a top priority for school leaders and the additional challenges it poses for school leaders to meet the rising mental health needs of students.

4 The Impact of the Youth Mental Health Crisis on Schools

The mental health crisis among the school-aged population has continued to escalate over the past few years. As articulated in previous chapters, the frequency and intensity of mental health issues among school-aged children have risen. The pandemic further exacerbated this trend and disproportionately impacted students psychosocially.[1] The level of unmet need has reached a breaking point for schools that work to support students with limited staff, programs, and resources. The inability to meet students' lower-level needs has resulted in more students elevating to higher levels of needs, which schools are often ill-equipped to manage. This chapter delves more deeply into the impact of the mental health crisis in schools.

Talk to anyone who works with young people, and they will quickly lament the change that they have seen, regardless of the length of their career, in the mental health of students. The concerns existed pre-pandemic but seemed to have reached a crescendo during and post-pandemic. The overall proportion of student support and the level of intensity have both been dramatically increasing.

During the pandemic, students' needs peaked. Districts worked to respond to meet those needs but were impacted by two realities: limited workforce/staffing as well as fiscal challenges. The inability to meet students' needs created a self-perpetuating cycle of increased needs that quickly overwhelmed the already challenged services available in schools and the fragile mental health care system.

During the pandemic, additional federal funding provided support to schools and districts as they worked to manage the pandemic's implications. Some schools use those resources to support students' mental health and social-emotional needs. Other schools and districts planned to use these additional resources in this way but were challenged to find staff to fulfill the plans. In typical times, large areas of the country have few, if any, local clinical providers and clinically trained school counselors or psychologists are scarce.[2] At a time of heightened need during the pandemic, this scarcity only increased.

A review of the first round of federal funding that was disbursed to support school districts during the pandemic found a range of uses for the additional funds. Since the sunsetting of additional funds, there has been a decline in districts' ability to meet students' needs. A 2024 survey from the National Center for Education Statistics reports that 48 percent of surveyed schools said that they were able to effectively provide mental health services to all students with needs, which is a decline from 2021–2 of 56 percent.[3] The latest survey also demonstrated a decrease in the use of grant funds to support mental health services, 37 percent, down from 53 percent in the 2021–2 school year.

That same survey also asked about barriers to meeting the needs of students. Results from the survey showed the three most common reasons that limit a school's ability to provide mental health care services to students. These included lack of staff (55 percent), insufficient funding (54 percent) and limited access to mental health professionals (49 percent).

Taken collectively, this presents a stark reality of the available resources to meet students' needs. Even with additional resources to districts, many districts could not implement support to meet students' needs. The impact is that a significant portion of student mental health needs are untreated, resulting in a negative impact on educational outcomes. Districts must work to expand resources to address student mental health needs more comprehensively. Not doing so will result in the consequences of untreated students within their schools and classrooms.

The Impact

As shared, concerns around student mental health have increased among school and district leaders over the recent past. Many feel helpless and unsure of how to act to better support students. Meanwhile, as the prevalence and intensity of mental health issues have increased, there has been a negative impact on the individual students who are not being effectively supported, the faculty and staff in schools, and the overall school climate.

The Student

Students struggling with mental health challenges experience a range of impacts on their school experience, including poorer academic performance. Academic impacts include difficulty concentrating or completing work and poor overall grades. There are also nonacademic impacts that are contributory to the challenges. Nonacademic impacts include difficulty connecting in school and making friends, excessive absences, and increased disciplinary interactions.

Students with identified learning differences suffer an even greater impact. Students with identified learning disabilities are more likely to suffer from anxiety than their typical peers.[4] Unsupported mental health issues create barriers to student learning and socialization that can have cascading impacts over time. Negative self-perception, low self-esteem, disengagement and disinterest in learning, and a lack of engagement in school activities are all possible impacts on student mental health.

As practitioners, we have seen countless examples of this cycle that can persist for unsupported students for years. A student with mental health challenges struggles to engage and complete academic work. They miss more school and are not connected socially to school. This lack of success often further exacerbates their mental health issues, which then have a deeper negative impact on academic achievement. This cycle will continue unless interventions are put in place that support the student around both mental health, academic, and social support.

Impact on Staff and School Climate

We have all experienced the significant impact an individual student or group of students can have on the school climate, both positively and negatively. As the number of students with unsupported mental health needs has risen, so has the level of challenging behavior. We all understand that it is not only those students with mental health challenges who are impacting the culture. The impact of the pandemic on typical social development among students, along with the powerful and often negative impact of social media, is also a contributing factor. These issues have, however, converged to create challenges in our schools at all levels.

The impact has been deeply felt by faculty and staff. There is a constant drumbeat about the challenges of teaching today. The pandemic amplified concerns. Many teachers share concerns about students' academic progress and behaviors. A majority of teachers, in a national survey, reported that they have to address behavioral issues in their classrooms regularly. They also cited anxiety and depression as a major problem among students at all levels.[5]

Teachers are generally less hopeful and optimistic about their ability to impact the lives of students. Their work has become increasingly difficult, with little relief on the horizon. The result has been an exodus from the profession, an unwillingness to recommend teaching as a profession to others, and lower matriculation of teacher candidates at colleges and universities.

The impact on the overall culture is also significant. School staff, at all levels, are reacting and responding to increased challenges of students exacerbated by unmet needs. They are doing more with less as additional funds that were available during and immediately following the pandemic evaporated. Many schools and districts have seen reductions in staffing since the pandemic. In this environment, engaging proactively to meet the needs of students is very difficult, which leads to burnout and decreased job satisfaction for school staff.

School Leaders' Perspective

In addition to the broadened need for support, schools have had difficulty meeting the increasing intensity of student needs. A 2023 national survey of parents and school administrators reported that nearly 90 percent of school administrators described the mental health challenges as moderate or severe.[6] This survey supports reports from the field that describe difficult and untenable circumstances in schools.

Principals also recognize the school's responsibility to meet the needs of students. Most principals recognize that social-emotional health and well-being are "very important" for academic success. Further, they estimate that up to 20 percent of students need prevention or intervention services.[7]

School and district leaders also recognize the enormous additional burden this places on them and other professionals within schools. However, they also recognize the importance of the schools and districts taking responsibility for providing additional mental health care support for students. They believe that schools are well positioned to identify and support the mental health needs of students if adequate resources are provided.

A report by EAB demonstrated that the sense of responsibility for supportive programming has shifted since prior to the pandemic. The report demonstrated that nearly 90 percent of superintendents somewhat or strongly agreed that schools have the responsibility to provide this support to students. While this belief has broadened, action to build additional support for students is largely unfulfilled.[2]

Similarly, at the building level, there is a heightened awareness of the collective responsibility to identify and/or provide support for students. Principals emphasized that one of the most important issues they face in their work with students includes working to increase awareness of mental health issues, to identify those in need of services, and to support students in gaining access to services.[7] For both school and district leaders, the recognition of the importance of engaging in this work is met with school structures that are not equipped to meet the needs of students.

As demonstrated, student mental health issues are a significant concern of school and district leaders. With existing structures in schools, districts have had difficulty in implementing effective changes to support students' increasing and evolving needs. Schools and districts, as organizations, tend to maintain the same staffing and programmatic practices over time. Any additions or changes in models are difficult and require additional fiscal resources.

Even with additional fiscal resources, influencing changes in these structures is complicated and difficult. This is further complicated by the traditional view of some community decision-makers that supporting student mental health is not the responsibility or purview of schools.

We must work intentionally to change that mindset. Schools must take responsibility for supporting the mental health of their students.

Accepting Our Responsibility

As discussed extensively, student mental health is at a critical point. The frequency and intensity of student mental health concerns have been on an increasing trajectory, which was amplified during the pandemic. While the data seems to indicate that a peak occurred during and immediately after the pandemic, student needs continue to go unmet. The impact is that schools are reacting to urgent student needs and using available services to support students who are in the most critical need. The result is that students with lower-level needs are often not having their needs met. Failing to meet the lower-level needs of students results in some students moving to a higher level of need.

The urgency of need has often outpaced a school's, and the broader child mental health care system's, ability to effectively support all students. Schools must act. Schools are best positioned to increase and enhance services for students to more effectively address these concerns. Schools have the ability to broaden responsibility to ensure that there is strong coordination and collaboration to improve student services. This can be accomplished through effective planning, partnership, innovation, and additional funding. In doing so, schools can make a tangible difference in improving support, and coordination of support, for students with mental health needs.

Meeting the mental health needs of students has become our collective responsibility. If schools are able to make the changes necessary to improve support, we can impact outcomes for students and change their trajectories. Schools can reduce the negative impacts of untreated mental health issues that keep educators up at night. Schools can deal with concerns at the earliest onset, thereby improving the likelihood of a positive outcome.

While meeting the needs of individual students is reason enough to engage, doing so will also result in significant positive impacts on schools. The overall school climate, reduction of disruptive behaviors, improved job satisfaction of teaching staff, and improved academic outcomes are all possible when we intentionally work to improve support for student mental health issues.

Key Takeaways

- Student mental health issues have continued to increase in both frequency and intensity among all groups of school-aged children.
- The current system and structure have been overwhelmed and are not able to effectively meet the needs of all students.

- The complexity of the child mental health care system and the lack of available personnel result in long delays before more intensive support and treatment is provided for students.
- Untreated student mental health issues are having a significant negative impact on those students and the larger school culture.
- Education leaders recognize their responsibility to expand support for students.
- Schools must act and expand support to meet the needs of all students, those at lower levels of need as well as those with more intensive needs.
- An improved level of support will improve outcomes for students and impact the overall school culture.

What's Next?

The responsibility to act is clear, but where do we begin? Through the re-engagement and expansion of a strong framework—Multi-Tiered Systems of Support (MTSS), school leaders will be able to begin to plan and implement changes. The next chapter provides an overview of the MTSS model and shares an expansion to Tier 4 to provide greater clarity about the type of programs and supports that schools need to embrace to improve success in supporting the mental health needs of all students.

Part II
An Expanded Planning Framework

5 The MTSS Framework and Tier 4

Every educator knows the acronym MTSS, which stands for Multi-Tiered System of Support. Within the education field, these four letters represent an approach to supporting students using three distinct tiers of education and intervention. In this chapter, we will provide a brief overview of the history of MTSS and their application to support student mental health issues. We will also introduce the addition of Tier 4 and discuss the rationale for inclusion by public schools to support students' social-emotional health.

A Brief History

A tiered prevention model is a product of the field of public health. The use of tiered interventions includes universal interventions (Tier 1), targeted interventions (Tier 2), and intensive interventions (Tier 3). An example from public health includes the campaign around reducing tobacco use. The tiered model applied to this issue included an education campaign to share the dangers of tobacco use (Tier 1), increasing smoke-free spaces (Tier 2), and providing resources to help people quit using tobacco (Tier 3).

Borrowing the framework from public health, MTSS were popularized in the field of education in the late 1990s. It increased in widespread use after the inclusion of PBIS (Positive Behavior Intervention and Supports) and RTI (Response to Intervention) within the Individuals with Disabilities Act in 1997 and 2004, respectively. MTSS was formally included in the Every Student Succeeds Act (ESSA) in 2015.[1] The inclusion of the MTSS framework in federal legislation resulted in most states requiring the use of this framework to support students.

An Overview of MTSS

MTSS is a framework that traditionally includes three tiers of intervention. The tiers are designed to support the varying needs of students by targeting supports based on the level of need. The MTSS framework has been adopted to include both academic and behavioral support. The goal is that by using targeted and appropriate levels of support for students, a school can meet the students' needs, which will then remove barriers to achievement. The MTSS framework also serves as a useful planning tool to ensure that there are appropriate supports at each tier within the framework.

It is important that identified supports exist at each tier to meet the wide range of needs within the student population. The model relies on the expectation that Tier 1 supports are available to all students, while Tiers 2 and 3 are available to a smaller targeted group of students. The absence of support in any of the tiers will impact the overall effectiveness of the tiered approach.

Imagine a partially implemented system where a tier does not exist. As an example, ineffective Tier 1 (universal) support will result in an increased number of students requiring support at Tiers 2 and 3. Connected, a sign of ineffective or nonexistent Tier 1 support is a higher number of students who have Tier 2 needs. However, if effectively implemented, support at each of the tiers will help to ensure that each student's needs are met and that a school can effectively manage the needs of students.

Tier 1 of the MTSS model is often called universal support. These supports are available to all students. In the academic framework, this includes the core curriculum and supports that a teacher would provide to differentiate instruction to meet students' needs. In the behavioral area, universal support would include the implementation of a program like Responsive Classroom. Whether academic or behavioral, all students have access to and exposure to the approach through their core experiences. An important goal is to have strong Tier 1 support which helps to prevent some students from pushing to higher-tiered needs.

Tier 2 of the MTSS model includes targeted interventions. These interventions are designed for students who are not meeting expectations despite their participation in Tier 1 universal support. Interventions in this tier are typically short-term and time-bound. For many practitioners, Tier 2 supports are planned with a specific length of time for which the intervention will be applied (e.g., six or eight weeks).

Some examples of Tier 2 academic support include differentiated instruction and curriculum supports or small group math intervention. For behavioral support, some examples may include implementing the Check-In Check-Out model, a "lunch bunch," or participation in small group counseling to provide specific behavioral interventions.

In Tier 3, intensive support is provided. These supports are typically implemented for the long-term, in comparison to Tier 2. Intensive support for students with academic challenges includes specialized education via special education services, one-on-one tutoring, or outside-of-class reading intervention, as a few examples. For behavioral support, some examples of intensive support include the development of Individualized Behavior Intervention Plans or participation in one-on-one counseling with a mental health clinician.

Another important feature of the MTSS framework is the identification of which tier students would fall on so that interventions can be matched to their needs. Practitioners are undoubtedly familiar with the MTSS pyramid, which provides a visual representation of the MTSS model. In this representation, universal interventions form the base and include all students. Each subsequent tier includes fewer students. Generally, it is expected that within a population of students, there is a proportion of students who fall within each tier. Figure 5.1 represents the typical MTSS triangle and the theoretical proportion of students who would fall in each tier.

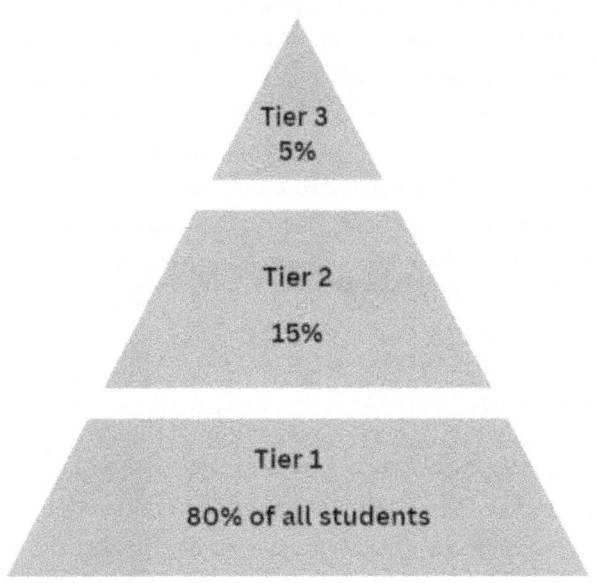

Figure 5.1 MTSS Tier 3 SEL model.

As shown in the figure, it is anticipated that approximately 80 percent of the student population will require only Tier 1—universal support. The number of students in Tier 2 is anticipated to be between 10 and 15 percent of the population, with about 5–10 percent of the population requiring Tier 3 support. As mentioned, this is a theoretical breakdown. For many schools, the proportions expressed are aspirational and not actual. Further, the mental health crisis among school-aged children has resulted in much higher proportions of students requiring Tier 2 and 3 interventions.

When reviewing the triangle, approaches to support student mental health fall into one of the three tiers that have been outlined. Some examples of programming within each tier of the traditional MTSS model are provided in the table below.

Tier 1 (Universal Supports)	Tier 2 (Intervention)	Tier 3 (Intensive Support)
K-12 Health and physical education program Social and emotional learning (SEL) programming School counseling curriculum Psychoeducation lessons with mental health disorder screening (i.e., Signs of Suicide) (secondary) Positive behavioral interventions and supports	Small group counseling Individualized skill-building activities Individualized counseling Check-in check-out program Digital mental health interventions such as individual learning modules Check and connect mentoring *typically short-term	Specialized social and emotional learning placements

Time for an Expanded MTSS Model

As outlined at length in Chapter 2, the mental health crisis among school-aged children is significant. With an increasing number of students exhibiting mental health challenges, school resources often fall short of meeting needs. To further complicate this reality, the intensity of need has also increased. The result has been that school districts have been unable, despite significant efforts, to meet the needs of students due to the number of students who have higher-tiered needs.

Many districts have attempted to resolve this by continuing to add staff to provide additional resources within schools. This takes the form of hiring additional school counselors, adjustment counselors, social workers, and school psychologists. In many areas throughout the country, the desire of a school district to hire additional personnel is met by the reality of staffing shortages in these critical need areas. This results in inadequate staffing to support the number and intensity of student needs.

To further complicate the challenge, many students are exhibiting an increased intensity of needs. This increased intensity results in schools supporting those students at the highest tier of need by providing an increased level of service, both in service time and intensity. The resources that have been redeployed to support students at the most critical state are then no longer available to support students at lower tiers.

A result of this redeployment of staff is that there are fewer available supports in the lower tiers. The needs of those students at lower tiers are not being effectively met. Some of those students who would have been well served by lower-tier support then move to requiring higher-tier support. Essentially, the combination of challenges—increasing student proportion and intensity and staffing challenges—have resulted in working within a "treatment-only" model, which does not prevent ascension to a higher level of support through early intervention (typically part of Tier 2).

This circumstance creates an untenable challenge for school and district leaders. It also results in a more costly, resource-intensive approach to meet students' needs. Resources must be directed to those students with the highest exhibited need, but doing so means that resources to change the trajectory of a student at risk—preventing them from elevating to the necessary level of support—will result in a larger number of students who require intensive support. This cycle is one in which many schools and districts find themselves taking deliberate action to alter.

A Revised Model

As discussed, the long-standing MTSS model has been developed with three clearly articulated tiers. The model serves as a guide for school and district leaders to identify levels of support based on student needs. The model, as currently constructed, however, presumes that intensive support, which typically occurs outside of school, will be met through a well-developed and well-executed pediatric mental health care system.

As we know, and as discussed in Chapter 3, with the increase in the proportion and intensity of students who need support, the pediatric mental health care system is overwhelmed and not functioning well. Often, school clinicians report weeks or months of waitlists for students to see outside-of-school clinicians to have their needs met. This current circumstance is untenable and unfair to the students that schools are working to support. So what is the answer?

One possible answer to help improve this current context is to shift the model by adopting a Tier 4 to the already existing MTSS model. In this revised model, Tier 4 is created to provide schools and districts with an understanding of their responsibility to support students outside the framework of schools and what has traditionally been within their locus of control.

Specifically, Tier 4 provides clarity that typical outside-of-school services, and the coordination of those, are the direct responsibility of the school and district. By accepting this responsibility, schools can develop and build a comprehensive support program for students. Schools are able to take control of the comprehensive support provided to students.

In doing so, schools are no longer subjected to a failure point when an outside-of-school provider cannot be located or the length of time before intensive support begins is weeks or months. The shift in the locus of control provides both a comprehensive and timely response to student needs. Thus improving the overall support and removing some barriers to student support.

The adoption of Tier 4 within the MTSS framework signals the responsibility of a district to coordinate or provide services for students that will take place outside of school—in private settings and with key partners. By assuming this increased level of responsibility, districts will also increase their control over the type and quality of support for students who previously were left to a system that is challenged and overwhelmed.

What Does a Tier 4 MTSS Model Look Like?

The addition of Tier 4 to the traditional MTSS model denotes a significant shift in the district's responsibility to support students comprehensively.

When Tier 4 is added to the traditional MTSS model, Tier 3 becomes divided. The addition of Tier 4 provides a more nuanced differentiation between the needs of students in Tier 3. In this adapted model, Tier 3 represents intensive support that is located within schools and supported by traditional school counseling personnel through emotional impairment-based individualized education programs (IEPs). Tier 4 denotes two areas of enhanced and intensive support, which are typically outside a district's locus of control.

First are those supports that are explicitly outside of typical school support but are supported, coordinated, and activated by the school. These include mental health care coordination and ongoing individual outpatient therapy. The second is the district's development of a wraparound team. This distinction is not about when the intensive support takes place but by whom the support is being delivered.

For example, imagine a student who is working with a school-based clinician when the level of concern and need rises. In the Tier 4 model, as the student's needs increase beyond what the school-based clinician can support, that clinician coordinates referrals and services so that the student can be seen by outside providers quickly and in coordination with what is occurring in school, potentially in addition to and in partnership with what is taking place in schools.

As described, the current Tier 3 model divides interventions by universal supports (Tier 1), interventions (Tier 2), and intensive supports (Tier 3). The addition of Tier 4 is essentially a subset of Tier 3 supports, which are coordinated by the school/district but typically occur outside of school and are necessary for students with highly intense needs. These supports are created through programs and partnerships established by the school/district to remove barriers to higher levels of support than are typically experienced.

This change to add Tier 4 to the well-known MTSS pyramid accomplishes two things. First, as stated, it divides Tier 3 to differentiate between "in-school IEP-directed services" and typically "out-of-school" mental health interventions. Second, it realigns the anticipated proportion of students at each tier, as seen in Figure 5.2 below.

As shown above, the expanded MTSS model accomplishes two things. First, it includes Tier 4. In addition, it realigns the proportion of students at

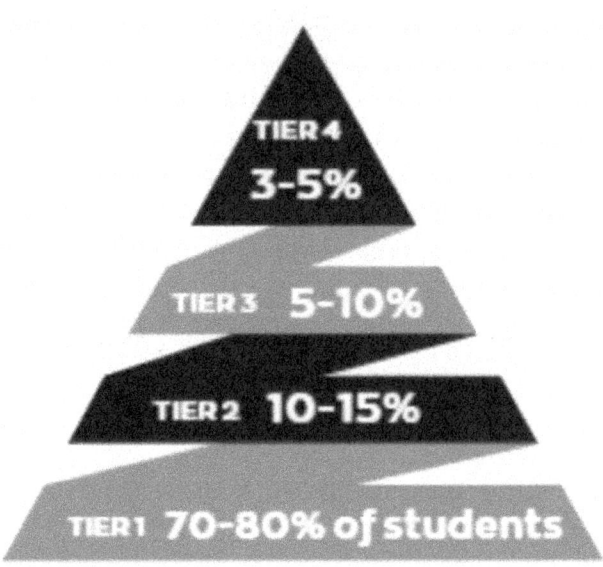

Figure 5.2 Expanded MTSS SEL model with Tier 4.

each tier. This is done to more closely approximate the number of students requiring each level of intervention so that districts can plan accordingly. In this updated model, 70–80 percent are at Tier 1, 10–15 percent at Tier 2, 5–10 percent at Tier 3, and 3–5 percent at the added Tier 4. In creating a more realistic proportion of students at each tier, districts can plan more effectively to support students by aligning resources to needs.

Key Takeaways

- The MTSS model is an important framework for schools to plan student support.
- The MTSS model's theoretical proportion of students at each tier does not take into consideration the student mental health crisis.
- The addition of Tier 4 to the traditional MTSS provides a targeted means to identify student needs.
- The updated Tier 4 model realigns the proportion of students at each tier.

What's Next?

The next chapter will provide a deeper dive into the MTSS Tier 4 model, including a discussion of the specific components of Tier 4. An examination of the limitations of a Tier 3 model will be further explored, as well as the rationale and benefits for expansion to a Tier 4 model are also explored. Through the use of a student scenario, Oliver, a broader discussion of the elements of Tier 4 and the use cases will be examined. Further, more specific examples of what constitutes Tier 4 will be shared throughout the chapter.

6 What Is MTSS Tier 4, and Why Do Schools Need It?

Within this chapter, we'll introduce you to Oliver, a student who is in need of mental health support. Oliver's school operates like most but utilizes the traditional MTSS three-tiered model and outpatient referrals to support students. We'll ask you to reflect on Oliver's situation and revisit his case study at the end of the chapter. Additionally, within this chapter, we'll examine the current challenges associated with the traditional school practices of relying on a three-tiered MTSS system and outpatient referrals to support student mental health. This examination will include exploring the limitations of MTSS Tier 3 and the current challenges with the pediatric mental health system. Let's start by getting to know Oliver and examining the limitations of the MTSS Tier 3 model.

The Story of Oliver

September and October

Oliver is starting the first grade this year. Like his classmates, he is eager to meet his teacher and new classmates. Other than a few minor and typical miscues, Oliver sails through the first few months of school. By all accounts, he appears to be making friends and can follow most classroom rules with only minor redirection.

November

As classroom expectations increase and social groups form, Oliver exhibits new behaviors. His teacher notices that he is having difficulty sitting at his desk and frequently reminds him to return to his chair. His teacher must also often stop "circle time" on the rug to help Oliver calm down.

December

By December, Oliver's behavior has become frequently disruptive. His teacher's strategies that had been working to help Oliver calm down and focus are no longer effective. In fact, his teacher has called the safety team several times to escort Oliver out of the room. As a result, Oliver's teacher refers him to their school's Instructional Support Team.

January

Oliver's teacher brings the strategies she's tried to use to support Oliver's behaviors and the patterns of his behavior that she has documented to the Instructional Support Team meeting. The team reviews the data and believes there is enough evidence to evaluate Oliver to determine his eligibility for an Individualized Education Program (IEP). Meanwhile, as his behaviors become more frequent, other students have become less likely to engage with Oliver, and he is often seen playing alone on the playground.

Oliver's school adjustment counselor believes he is exhibiting behaviors consistent with an anxiety disorder. She shares this with his parents, who ask Oliver to be seen at school for counseling. With apologies, his adjustment counselor shared that she can only see students with IEPs due to caseload restrictions. They both agree that the best course of action is to take Oliver to the pediatrician to be evaluated while they wait for the IEP process to conclude.

February/March

Over the next two months, the special education team at Oliver's school collects data and observes Oliver's behaviors and academic performance. Due to a high volume of evaluations and limited staff, the evaluation process takes nearly forty-five days. In the meantime, Oliver's parents take him to see his pediatrician. Oliver's pediatrician listens to him and his parents and even gets a release to speak to his school adjustment counselor. His pediatrician concludes that Oliver is likely dealing with an anxiety disorder but is uncomfortable prescribing medication to a young child, and she does not have the training or time to provide in-office therapy. Therefore, his pediatrician makes two referrals: one for a child psychiatrist and a second for outpatient therapy. Oliver is placed on a waitlist for both services.

April

Oliver's IEP evaluation cycle has concluded, and the special education team has found that Oliver has an emotional disturbance that negatively impacts his academic performance. A meeting will occur at the month's end to create an IEP for Oliver. Oliver is still waiting to be seen by an outpatient therapist and a psychiatrist. Due to holding public insurance, the wait to see a psychiatrist is six to nine months long, and for an outpatient therapist is four to six months long.

May/June

With an IEP in place, Oliver is now eligible for Tier 3 counseling services. In this case, his IEP calls for him to meet for counseling with the school adjustment counselor once a week. Due to her heavy caseload, Oliver has his first session in mid-May. Oliver can meet with the school adjustment counselor for three sessions before the summer break. He is still waiting for an appointment with an outpatient therapist and psychiatrist.

Reflection Questions

Please keep the following questions in mind as you read this chapter. We will return to them to provide insights at the end of the chapter:

1. What are the limitations of the MTSS Tier 3 system of support?
2. What are the limitations of the current pediatric outpatient mental health system?
3. How did these limitations affect Oliver and his family?
4. How was Oliver's social, emotional, and academic growth impacted by these systematic limitations?
5. What could be done differently to better support Oliver?

Limitations of MTSS Tier 3

As outlined in Chapter 4, MTSS Tier 3 can effectively support students with documented, through the IEP process, emotional impairments or behavioral concerns. Often, Tier 3 services recommended through the IEP process focus on individual counseling provided during the school day by a school adjustment counselor or school social worker. Although it is imperative to offer Tier 3 social and emotional school services, the orientation for providing services is reactionary, the process for receiving services is laborious, and the scope of services is limited.

A Reactionary Approach to Support

Tier 3 social and emotional services are designed to support 1–5 percent of the student population. As we have shared, the percentage of students who would benefit from these types of intensive mental health services is, in reality, much more significant. One of the reasons this discrepancy exists is the way in which students are identified as needing Tier 3 support.

By definition, students recommended for Tier 3 services have not responded to interventions in either Tier 1 or Tier 2, typically because they have needs that exceed what the other tiers can provide. As a result, students referred to Tier 3 have usually shown signs of needing additional support for long periods of time that generally manifest as outward behaviors. Unfortunately, one of the most efficient ways for students to be identified and referred for Tier 3 services is when their social and emotional needs become disruptive. Some of the most common examples of Tier 3 behaviors include:

- Chronic social and emotional classroom disruptions
- Ongoing office referrals for discipline
- Suspensions and other removals from the classroom
- Dangerous or highly disruptive behaviors
- Behaviors that result in social or physical isolation

These disruptive behaviors are easily identified by educators, and due to the upheaval the behaviors cause, these students are often fast-tracked for a Tier 3 referral. This reactionary approach to identifying students needing Tier 3 support can leave students who are struggling with social and emotional issues but displaying inward behaviors largely unnoticed until times of crisis.

Due to the reactionary nature of the Tier 3 identification and referral process, a high percentage of students' social and emotional needs go undetected and unsupported. For example, a student grappling with depression may experience changes in their eating habits, sleeping patterns, energy levels, and ability to concentrate. However, none of these behavior changes will disrupt the continuity of a classroom or school environment and, therefore, do not often rise to the level of a Tier 3 referral until a crisis occurs.

A student experiencing severe mental health concerns with inward-facing symptoms may go unnoticed until a drastic change in behavior that grabs the attention of adults takes place. This behavior change often manifests as school refusal, self-harm activity, or suicidal ideation. These outward warning signs often translate into a school mental health professional conducting an evaluation or risk assessment. This triggering behavior change and subsequent assessment most often lead to a Tier 3 referral and utilization of support services. In addition to the reactionary approach to making Tier 3 referrals being a limiting factor for students receiving Tier 3 services, the pace at which referrals are made and services are rendered is also a limitation of the MTSS Tier 3 model. This long-standing approach is explored in the next section.

A Sloth-Like Approach to Receiving Supports

Traditionally, Tier 3 social and emotional supports are reserved for students with an Individualized Education Program (IEP). An IEP is a written legal document that maps out a program of specialized supports and services students need to make progress to thrive in school. IEPs are important because they help to ensure that students get what they need to succeed in school; however, these individualized plans require a great deal of resources and are, therefore, limited to students with specific needs.

According to the US Department of Education's Individuals with Disabilities Education Act, a student is eligible for an IEP under emotional disturbance if he/she exhibits one or more of the following characteristics over a long period of time and to a marked degree, which adversely affects educational performance:

1. An inability to learn that cannot be explained by intellectual, sensory, or health factors;
2. An inability to build or maintain satisfactory interpersonal relationships with peers and teachers;
3. Inappropriate types of behavior or feelings under normal circumstances exhibited in several situations;
4. A general pervasive mood of unhappiness or depression; and
5. A tendency to develop physical symptoms or fears associated with personal or school problems.

To determine eligibility for an IEP and Tier 3 social and emotional services, a student must go through a lengthy process that consists of a referral, evaluation, eligibility determination, IEP development, and IEP implementation. The very length of this process and lack of any intervention may result in a student who would have been on the cusp of needing Tier 3 services being identified as clearly needing these specialized supports.

To receive social and emotional Tier 3 services, a student is first referred for a formal evaluation. This referral usually comes from a teacher or a parent. Often, the referral is considered by a team's Instructional Support Team before the student is formally evaluated. The evaluation phase must be conducted within forty-five days of receiving parental consent to evaluate a student. During the evaluation phase, data is collected in all areas of concern: social, emotional, and academic. The data collected is used to determine student eligibility for services.

After the evaluation is complete, an eligibility determination is conducted. For a student to receive services for a mental health impairment or emotional disturbance, the evaluation must show that the student has a disability and that the disability is affecting academic and/or functional performance. If the student meets these requirements, a meeting will take place to develop their IEP. This meeting must be conducted within thirty days of the eligibility determination. Finally, after the IEP is developed, the student's services must be put in place as soon as possible, but it can take up to thirty days.

All told, it can often take up to 195 days for a student to be identified as having a mental health concern that qualifies them to receive Tier 3 support services, as seen in Figure 6.1. Keep in mind a school year is typically ~180 days in the United States. This process is intentionally detailed and lengthy

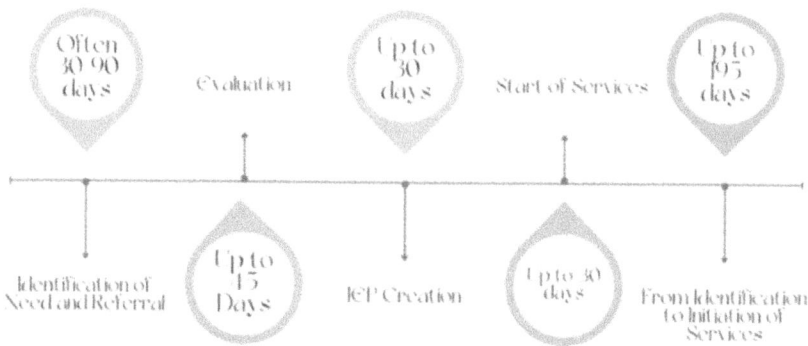

Figure 6.1 MTSS Tier 3 timeline.

to ensure that only those students most in need of support receive it. Many would suggest that this approach is necessary for the MTSS model because Tier 3 services need to be limited due to limited resources.

Often, schools have one clinician who is licensed to deliver Tier 3 behavioral disturbance IEP services. These intensive one-on-one services take up a great deal of time and, therefore, constrain the clinician's caseload to around a maximum of thirty students. Furthermore, these services must be delivered during the school day and most often occur on school grounds. As a result, students needing intensive mental health support must wait months to be seen by a school clinician, which can feel like an eternity for them and their parents/guardians during a crisis. As a result, school systems have traditionally looked to outpatient mental health services to support students in ways they cannot.

Challenges with the Outpatient Referral Model

The traditional approach of schools referring students who do not qualify for Tier 3 services to outpatient pediatric mental health services is no longer effective. As detailed in Chapters 1 and 3 of this book, the significant rise of adolescent mental health needs coupled with the systematic challenges of the outpatient pediatric mental health care model have completely sunk this once effective approach to supporting student mental health needs. To create effective pediatric outpatient mental health systems, layers of change must take place.

Some of these complex changes include attracting more mental health professionals into the field, increasing reimbursement for outpatient services, and providing incentives for treating patients with public health insurance. While these changes would certainly impact the root cause of the inefficiencies of the pediatric outpatient mental health model, they will likely take decades to resolve. In the meantime, outpatient pediatric mental health providers will continue to be incentivized to provide telehealth services to families willing to pay out of pocket.

For these reasons, school systems must begin to support student mental health needs differently. We believe the most effective, efficient, and sustainable approach to better supporting student mental health needs in school is to incorporate a Tier 4 social and emotional level of support into the

MTSS model. In the next section, we'll introduce the concept of a Tier 4 MTSS model, but while the limitations of the MTSS Tier 3 model and the outpatient pediatric mental health system are fresh in your mind, let's revisit the case of Oliver.

Revisiting the Case of Oliver

To start this chapter, we asked you to keep several reflection questions in mind about Oliver and his experience within the current MTSS and pediatric mental healthcare model. We also asked you to consider how this interaction impacted his well-being. We'll revisit those questions now with some of our reflections:

What are the limitations of the MTSS Tier 3 system of support?

There were several limitations to MTSS Tier 3 supports exhibited in the case of Oliver. In Oliver's experience, like most students, he was identified as having mental health concerns through outward behaviors that took months to manifest. However, if Oliver was dealing with a mental health concern that didn't manifest as disruptive behavior, it may have taken much longer for Oliver to be referred for an IEP evaluation. This limitation displays the need for proactive mental health screening for students of all ages.

Another limitation displayed through this case is the time it takes from when a student begins to exhibit concerning symptoms until counseling services are rendered. This can potentially take an entire school year, if not longer. Additionally, most schools are only able to offer Tier 3 counseling support to students with IEPs due to budget and staffing constraints. This limitation was evident in Oliver's case, as the school adjustment counselor did not have the opportunity to provide one-on-one counseling with Oliver unless an IEP mandated it.

What are the limitations of the current pediatric outpatient mental health system?

When considering Oliver's case, we see a familiar situation play out. We have an engaged parent, school clinician, and pediatrician trying to do what is best for Oliver. However, due to limitations in their scope of practice and expertise, they are at the mercy of the outpatient mental healthcare system in order to fully treat Oliver. The problem with this is that there is a shortage of clinicians to support both medication management and ongoing therapy for pediatric patients such as Oliver.

This is compounded by the fact that his family carries public insurance, which offers low reimbursement rates to providers, making the pool of available clinicians even smaller. As a result, Oliver must wait four to nine months to be seen by the clinicians his pediatrician has referred him to.

How did these limitations affect Oliver and his family?

Of course, we don't know how the limitations of the MTSS Tier 3 and outpatient pediatric mental healthcare systems affected Oliver and his family, but we can hypothesize. Even with an engaged parent and helpful school clinician, the stress of being unable to support your child in need can weigh on a family. Likely, Oliver's untreated anxiety impacted his life at home and within the community. When anxiety manifests in the form of outward behaviors, it can naturally lead families to avoid places that trigger their child, even at the risk of social isolation for all family members. This type of "pull-back" reduces feelings of anxiety for the child and, as a result, reduces the prevalence of disruptive behaviors. However, this type of change in social patterns can perpetuate family stress and is to the detriment of the child's social and emotional growth.

How was Oliver's social, emotional, and academic growth impacted by these systematic limitations?

As you can imagine, untreated pediatric anxiety is likely to negatively impact the social, emotional, and academic growth of a child. This is true for Oliver. He ended the year well below grade level in both math and reading. This makes sense, as he was often removed from the classroom due to his behavioral interruptions. Additionally, when he was present in class, he found it difficult to focus and engage in the learning.

Oliver's social and emotional growth also suffered due to his anxiety. His frequent disruptive behavior made it challenging for him to interact with peers within the classroom. He often received modified instruction when his classmates formed small groups or engaged in "morning meeting" type activities as a full class. Furthermore, his behaviors led some of his classmates to avoid interacting with him in all areas of the school, including at recess and lunch. As a result, Oliver was robbed of a great deal of instructive and natural opportunities to authentically learn and practice social and emotional learning skills.

What could be done differently to better support Oliver?

In the absence of overhauling the entire MTSS Tier 3 and pediatric mental health system, there are several targeted changes that Oliver's school could make to better support students with his type of needs. First, if universal screening for social and emotional learning competencies and mental health concerns had been in place at Oliver's school, his underlying anxiety would have been identified much sooner, perhaps even before it was displayed through his outward behaviors.

Next, his school could have provided care coordination. This service could have greatly reduced the wait time for a clinician that Oliver experienced. Finally, his school could have offered in-school outpatient therapy. This, too, would have allowed Oliver to be paired with a therapist within weeks instead of waiting months. How these services can be integrated into an MTSS Tier 4 model will become much more clearer as we introduce the structure in the next section.

MTSS SEL Tier 4

As outlined thus far, the current MTSS model to support students' social, emotional, and mental health needs has three distinct tiers. Prior to the environmental changes affecting student mental health and the acceleratory event of the Covid-19 pandemic, the approach of using Tier 3 supports and referring students for outpatient mental health care was adequate. Unfortunately, this approach no longer addresses the growing prevalence and intensity of students' mental health needs and requires a more effective framework for schools to utilize.

Our systematic approach has been to create a fourth tier of support within the MTSS framework. However, upon a review of the literature, we discovered that little had been written about how to expand to a fourth tier of support. In fact, there are only a few instances of the concept of MTSS Tier 4 being piloted for academic support, but a search for MTSS Tier 4 SEL supports came up empty. Since it is our belief that adding MTSS SEL Tier 4 support has become essential when considering how to support student mental health, we've sought to create a framework that schools can use to implement a Tier 4 approach. This framework, which includes four core components, will be previewed in the next section and expanded upon in great detail in Chapter 8.

Essential Components of an MTSS Tier 4 Model

Tier 4 SEL supports should target students with critical mental health needs. This could mean students who are experiencing a mental health crisis, in need of post-crisis support, or are dealing with chronic mental health or social services concerns that are interfering with their ability to achieve academic success. Additionally, Tier 4 support should address the previously discussed barriers and limitations of the MTSS three-tiered model and outpatient pediatric mental healthcare system. To support this level of student need and to address systemic barriers, it is our belief that an MTSS Tier 4 model should include the following components:

1. Universal and targeted mental health screening.
2. Dedicated mental health care coordination.
3. In-school outpatient and/or tele-mental health therapy.
4. Wraparound mental health services.

Key Takeaways

- The MTSS Tier 3 system of support is reactionary and limited to supporting students with IEPs
- Once identified as needing Tier 3 support, the referral, eligibility, and IEP implementation process can take many months to complete.
- The pediatric outpatient mental health system is overloaded, and it typically takes months for the patients to have their initial appointment.
- The limitations of the MTSS Tier 3 and outpatient mental health system create large gaps in time between the identification of student needs and treatment.
- Instituting MTSS Tier 4 SEL supports can help improve how schools identify and support student mental health needs.

What's Next?

In the next chapter, we'll explain the elements of an MTSS Tier 4 model in great detail. We'll also share with you how to integrate these Tier 4 components into your current MTSS model. Before moving on, please take a moment to review the key takeaways.

7 Advantages of the Tier 4 Model

Resistance to systems change often stems from a deeply ingrained fear of the unknown. People naturally gravitate toward familiarity, and even when the current system has flaws, the prospect of stepping into uncharted territory can be daunting. As management expert Peter Drucker famously said, "People in any organization are always attached to the obsolete—the things that should have worked but did not, the things that once were productive and no longer are." This attachment to the status quo creates a significant barrier to embracing change, as the comfort of the known often outweighs the potential benefits of the unknown.

When contemplating the shift from the traditional three-tiered MTSS approach to adopting the Tier 4 model, school administrators will encounter multiple points of resistance. In fact, if you are a school administrator, you may be experiencing it right now, but dealing with the internal strife of whether it is worth departing from an obsolete but known system to a new and likely more effective way of supporting student mental health needs. One approach to pushing past this resistance is making sure that you and those who you will be collaborating with to institute a systems change understand the advantages of making the change before attempting it.

Fully grasping the advantages of adopting a Tier 4 Model will help to build motivation, reduce resistance, and provide a clear direction for the change process. Simon Sinek, a leadership expert and author, emphasized this consensus-building approach when he said, "People don't buy what you do; they buy why you do it." In this chapter, you will explore the benefits of adopting a Tier 4 approach to addressing student mental health, which include early identification of student needs, increased access to mental health and social services, increases in academic success, and fiscal efficiencies.

Student Benefits Associated with the Tier 4 Model

An Ounce of Mental Health Screening Is Worth a Pound of Cure

"Prevention is better than cure," as the saying goes, which holds true for student mental health. By identifying students' mental health needs early, schools can reduce learning loss, disruptive student behaviors, and the need for more intensive treatments. This proactive approach improves academic performance and fosters a healthier, more resilient student population.

Schools that implement regular social and emotional/mental health screenings can identify students who might be struggling and provide support before they fall behind academically or socially. One significant advantage is the early identification and support for students who might be struggling, which can prevent issues from escalating. For instance, a study by the *Journal of the American Academy of Child and Adolescent Psychiatry*, written by Dr. Jennifer G. Green of Boston University, found that schools with mental health resources focused on the early identification of student mental health needs saw a significant association with mental health service use for adolescents with mild/moderate mental and behavioral disorders.[1]

In addition to providing improved pathways to accessing mental health services, these screenings contribute to improved social outcomes. The National Institute of Mental Health highlights that early mental health intervention can reduce the likelihood of future mental health disorders.[2] Students who receive timely support are better equipped to develop strong social skills, leading to improved relationships with peers and teachers. For example, a report by the Center for School Mental Health found that schools practicing regular screenings saw a 21 percent decrease in reported bullying incidents and a 30 percent increase in student engagement in extracurricular activities.[3]

This holistic approach not only fosters a more supportive and inclusive school environment but also equips students with the resilience and coping skills necessary for long-term success. Proactive student screening, when paired with additional elements of the Tier 4 model, such as dedicated care coordination and enhanced access to outpatient therapy, can lead to the early identification and efficient treatment of student mental health concerns.

Increased Mental Health Access = Better Education

Studies show that half of all mental health disorders begin by age fourteen and three-quarters by age twenty-four.[4] The National Institute of Mental Health reports that early identification and treatment of pediatric mental health disorders can help children develop more effective coping strategies, leading to improved academic performance and social interactions.[4] One of the most significant benefits of instituting a Tier 4 model is an increase in mental health care access for students. This increase in mental health care access brings many advantages to students and schools, with the most impactful being an increase in student safety and better educational outcomes.

According to the Centers for Disease Control and Prevention, suicide is the second leading cause of death for individuals aged ten to twenty-four in the United States.[5] By providing greater access to mental health resources, schools can identify at-risk youth and offer necessary support and interventions. Research has shown that when children and adolescents have access to mental health services, particularly in a school-based setting, there is a marked decrease in suicide attempts and completions.[6] The addition of a Tier 4 program can increase access to mental health services in a convenient and familiar environment for students and families to seek help.

Moreover, increasing access to mental health services can lead to better educational outcomes. Mental health challenges such as anxiety, depression, and attention deficit hyperactivity disorder (ADHD) can significantly hinder a child's ability to focus, engage, and succeed in school. The American Psychological Association highlights that untreated mental health issues can lead to higher rates of absenteeism, disciplinary problems, and lower academic achievement.[7] Providing access to mental health support can help students manage their symptoms, leading to improved attendance, behavior, and grades.[8] This increase in mental health care services through the adoption of a Tier 4 program not only benefits students but also creates avenues for families to acquire mental health and social services more easily.

Wraparound Care Improves Student Outcomes

One of the hallmarks of a Tier 4 program is bringing mental health and social services support to the family through a wraparound model. The traditional MTSS structure centers access to support around school hours and the physical school building. However, for families and, by extension, students in need of mental health and social services, this approach lacks accessibility by creating barriers connected to taking time off of work, transportation, and negative past experiences in school. However, when schools can deliver these services within the home and community, several advantages emerge, including improved mental health outcomes, enhancements in academic performance, and increased family satisfaction.

Wraparound services are associated with significant improvements in mental health outcomes for youth, including reductions in emotional and behavioral problems. A study by Bruns and Suter found that youth receiving wraparound services showed significant improvements in emotional and behavioral functioning compared to those receiving traditional services. In fact, this study showed a 42 percent improvement in functioning among youth in wraparound programs.[9] Other research findings have indicated that children in wraparound care had fewer mental health symptoms and better functioning in school and home environments.[10] This enhanced functioning in school has been shown to improve student academic performance.

Dr. Martha Morrison Dore, researcher and professor of social work, once shared, "In-home social work services are crucial in providing a stable and supportive environment for children. These services address the unique needs of each family, resulting in significant improvements in children's emotional and behavioral health, academic performance, and overall well-being."[11] This sentiment certainly rings true when considering the academic advantages of instituting a Tier 4 model wraparound program.

In-home social work services, delivered through a Tier 4 model, can positively impact children's academic performance by addressing barriers to learning, such as family stress, poor home environments, and unmet mental health needs. This was shown in a study by Rones and Hoagwood, which found that children receiving in-home services had improved school attendance and academic performance.[12] Additionally, the addition of a therapeutic mentoring program, as part of a wraparound program, also can deliver significant advantages to a student's well-being.

A therapeutic mentor, as part of a Tier 4 wraparound program, works with students to develop social, coping, problem-solving, and communication skills to support their mental health. These skills are practiced and applied within the home and community settings to expedite their real-world application by students. As a result, students can better navigate life's challenges more successfully and reduce the likelihood of engaging in risky behaviors.[13] In addition to skill development, students who partner with therapeutic mentors have been shown to have improved mental health and academic outcomes.

Adolescents who work with therapeutic mentors often show significant improvements in their mental health. Specifically, mentoring relationships can reduce symptoms of depression and anxiety in youth and help adolescents cope with stressors and emotional challenges more effectively.[14] Therapeutic mentoring has also been linked to better academic outcomes. Research indicates that mentored youth are more likely to have improved grades, higher school attendance, and greater educational aspirations.[15] Therapeutic mentoring, as well as the other components of the Tier 4 model, offer many advantages to students and their families, and as a result, schools benefit as well.

School and District Benefits Associated with the Tier 4 Model

Supporting the mental health of even one student can have a ripple effect throughout the entire school community. When this effect is multiplied to dozens or even hundreds of students through the implementation of a Tier 4 program, entire schools and districts will feel the impact across multiple domains. Importantly, the domains likely to be impacted are those of the utmost importance to school administrators: student attendance, student behaviors, academic performance, and school finances.

Students with untreated mental health issues often exhibit higher absenteeism. Proactive mental health screening and increased access to mental health services help address these issues, leading to improved attendance.[16] In a review conducted by the National Center for School Mental Health, it was found that schools with comprehensive mental health programs, which have overlapping components of a Tier 4 model, saw a significant reduction in absenteeism rates.[17]

Additionally, by addressing home-based issues that affect school attendance, wraparound social work services can lead to improved attendance. Wraparound team members help identify barriers to attendance, such as family conflicts or transportation issues, and work with families to resolve them. The School Social Work Association of America reports that schools with active in-home social work programs see better attendance rates among students.[18] Similarly, incidents of student behaviors are shown to improve as a result of services provided within the Tier 4 model.

Proactive mental health screening helps in the early identification and intervention of mental health issues, leading to better management of behavioral problems. Studies have shown that early intervention can reduce the incidence of behavioral issues in students.[19] According to the National Alliance on Mental Illness, early intervention can prevent mental health conditions from worsening, leading to fewer disciplinary actions and improved classroom behavior.[20]

Likewise, the addition of wraparound services provides personalized support to students and their families, addressing issues that may contribute to negative behaviors. This tailored approach helps in reducing disruptive behaviors in school.[21] With rates of attendance increasing and incidents of student behaviors decreasing, it is not unfair to hypothesize that Tier 4 services would positively affect student academic performance, which they do.

Proactive mental health screening increases access to mental health services, which has a direct positive impact on academic performance. Early identification and intervention for mental health issues allow students to receive the support they need, leading to improved focus, engagement, and academic outcomes. According to the Centers for Disease Control and Prevention, students who receive mental health support show significant improvements in academic performance, including higher grades and test scores.[22]

This assertion was supported by a study published in the *Journal of School Psychology*, which found that students who received school-based mental health services demonstrated a 10 percent improvement in academic achievement compared to those who did not receive such services, and a report by the Substance Abuse and Mental Health Services Administration highlighted that early mental health intervention in schools can lead to a 20 percent increase in high school graduation rates.[23, 24] The academic outcomes connected to in-home wraparound services are very similar to those seen through the addition of student mental health screening and improved access to services.

In-home wraparound services address issues within the family and home environment that can affect a student's academic performance. Wraparound team members collaborate with families to create stable and supportive home environments, which in turn helps students focus better on their studies. According to the National Association of Social Workers, students receiving in-home social work support are more likely to complete homework, participate in class, and achieve higher academic results.[25]

This claim is backed up by research conducted by the Child Trends organization, which found that students who had access to in-home social work services experienced a 15 percent improvement in their overall academic performance.[26] Additionally, a study by the American Educational Research Association reported that schools implementing comprehensive in-home social work programs saw a 25 percent increase in student standardized test scores.[27] Although any school administrator would feel great about implementing a program that improves student attendance, behaviors, and academic achievement, they also must always consider the financial impact of adding services and staff.

The financial benefits of adding a Tier 4 program are multifaceted and, therefore, are more complicated to directly measure when compared to such markers as student attendance and academic performance. With that said, it has been found that by addressing mental health issues early, schools can reduce costs associated with disciplinary actions, special education services, and academic failure.[28, 29]

Additionally, the financial benefits of in-home wraparound services include reduced costs related to behavioral interventions, absenteeism, and special education services. By addressing issues at home, wraparound team members help prevent problems from escalating, leading to cost savings for schools. The Economic Policy Institute found that schools investing in social work services see a return on investment through improved student performance and reduced need for costly interventions.[30] If a school is willing to invest in a Tier 4 program, the research shows that they are not only likely to see a return on their financial investment but will also experience advantages related to student attendance, behaviors, and academics. Experiencing these advantages will make for a very appreciative staff, parent, and student school community.

Key Takeaways

- Proactive screening leads to the early identification of student mental health needs and expedited access to mental health services.
- Increased access to mental health services is associated with improvements in students' social and emotional skills.
- Increased access to mental health services is associated with a decrease in suicide attempts and completions.
- Increased access to mental health services is associated with increases in attendance, decreases in disciplinary problems, and increases in academic success.
- In-home wraparound mental health services are associated with improved mental health outcomes, enhancements in academic performance, and increased family satisfaction.
- The adoption of a Tier 4 model brings many advantages to a school district, including improvements in student attendance, student behaviors, academic performance, and school finances.

What's Next?

The next chapter discusses the development of Tier 4 supports, including proactive mental health screening, dedicated care coordination, in-school outpatient therapy, and wraparound mental health services. A deep discussion of each component includes an explanation of each, as well as the benefits and decision points for districts as they contemplate expanding support. In addition, "Oliver" returns as a case example of what Tier 4 services might look like at the individual student level.

Part III
Putting the Plan into Action

8 Planning for Success

A critical first step in any significant change effort is to ensure that implementation is effective by taking the necessary time to plan for change. It takes great discipline and patience to identify a path for improvement, and then the necessary time is taken to develop an implementation plan while also developing buy-in from stakeholders. Like all large-scale improvement efforts, achieving the goal will rest on the effectiveness of the well-constructed and comprehensive implementation plan. While the excitement of bringing enhanced mental health support to students is not an idea that should wait, an important first step in initiating a change process is to take the time to develop a specific implementation plan for the change effort.

Like any significant change process, identifying and implementing a comprehensive support system for student mental health is a multi-year process that will require intentionality, ongoing review, and revisions along the way. It is more than a list of actions and tasks to complete in a specific order. Instead, it is a change in practice, and likely beliefs of the organization, that will require ongoing nurturing, persistence, and flexibility to ensure success. It is a change in the organization's normative thinking about how we support student mental health.

If the implementation of this is done poorly, the impact may catastrophically delay your district's ability to engage in improvement. This chapter is not intended to outline a comprehensive change process. There are many excellent resources that exist that will guide the planning, development, and implementation of significant change processes. Those frameworks will provide an excellent roadmap to plan for change. Instead, the goal of this chapter is to share some additional considerations and identify pitfalls and steps that cannot be skipped when planning for change to help maximize the potential for success of this important change effort.

As educational leaders, we are compelled to act and engage in improvement efforts when we see that current structures and supports are not as effective. The instinct to jump in and begin making changes is admirable but can often result in creating challenges during implementation when they do not need to exist.

Often, leaders consider the specific actions, changes, and adjustments to practice that need to be made to meet with success. This alone, however, is not enough. In planning, we must consider the context of our programming by understanding both current conditions and the level of buy-in for the expansion of the work within schools, among officials, and within the broader community. Neglecting consideration of the level of buy-in and not planning a deliberate approach to improve buy-in will result in less effective change implementation.

When planning for this change, it is essential that you ensure engagement in the following areas to increase the likelihood of success of the change. Doing so will take more time, initially, than jumping right in, but will prevent problems as you begin implementation. Four essential considerations for your work include:

- Conducting an Environmental Scan
- Conducting a Needs Assessment
- Plan and Implement a Communication Strategy
- Building Support and Momentum

Conducting an Environmental Scan

An Environmental Scan is an important first step in this process. An Environmental Scan will provide you with valuable information to plan change and inform decision-making along the way.

An Environmental Scan is a specific process by which you gather information about the current context and "conditions on the ground," analyze the impact, and identify the internal and external factors that are impacting student mental health. By engaging in this process, you will be able to identify the elements that will impact the success of your change efforts. Without conducting an Environmental Scan, your efforts will be less efficient and less targeted at responding to the conditions on the ground.

An Environmental Scan will provide your organization with a deep understanding of the internal and external factors that support or hinder student mental health programming. Through an Environmental Scan, for example, you may find that your community has insufficient local resources to support student mental health. In conducting an Environmental Scan, it is important to engage in an authentic and honest review of conditions without critique or criticism. Doing so will result in an accurate review and understanding of current conditions.

Conducting an Environmental Scan will allow you to inventory the available resources, both within your school and outside, and begin to identify gaps and opportunities. Key components of an Environmental Scan include the following:

- Inventory Current Resources: Assemble a list of resources currently available in support of student mental health. It is helpful to organize these resources on the Expanded MTSS model, which will support the Needs Assessment phase of this work.
- Identify Improvement Opportunities: As you assemble the list of available resources, programmatic gaps, and opportunities will become visible.
- Assess Potential Threats: Identify those circumstances, structures, resources, attitudes, and beliefs that may prevent positive movement in improving resources for students.
- Identify Goals: While a more intensive identification of goals will take place as part of the Needs Assessment, this process will identify those highlighted areas of opportunity.

An effective Environmental Scan will set you up for success as you begin this work. The findings will help you pre-identify the potential challenges you will face. As discussed at the opening, gaining buy-in is an important aspect of initiating this work. A thorough Environmental Scan will help you to recognize the current beliefs and opinions of key players in decision-making as you move forward. Your identification of these groups and individuals will provide more time to help move them from a disagreement with this path toward supporting it.

The Needs Assessment

The next step of this important change process is to conduct a Needs Assessment. With the abundance of information and data that you uncovered during the Environmental Scan, the Needs Assessment will provide the opportunity for the team to dig deeper and begin to identify the specific needs of the population and which strategies will be used to meet those needs.

Conducting a Needs Assessment will require a systematic process of identifying and prioritizing the needs of students around mental health. Specifically, a needs assessment will look closely at both the big picture (Environmental Scan) and the specifics to identify and understand specific gaps or deficiencies that exist within programming for students. Similar to the Environmental Scan, it is helpful, in concert, to use the Expanded MTSS model to identify where current resources exist (which Tier) to help inform the decision-making around programmatic improvement.

Key steps in conducting a Needs Assessment include the following:

- Determine the Scope of the Assessment. The Environmental Scan should be helpful in framing what the Needs Assessment will dig deeper into to better understand.
- Data Gathering. This is a critical step. As you gather relevant data to better understand the needs of the student population, those metrics will often be those that you use to determine the success of the change process. During this step, you will likely need to identify and create an opportunity to collect data that has not been collected. It is important during this step to carefully consider how well the data collection will inform your decision-making now, as well as the utility of the data in demonstrating the impact of your change efforts.
- Data Analysis. With a well-engaged data collection effort, data analysis will help to refine your understanding of the needs of the group further. It will provide you with important information on the root causes related to these challenges.
- Develop an Action Plan. This is perhaps the most exciting part of this process. Finally, you are able to identify how you are going to make changes to improve the experience for students. As mentioned, this is the step that many groups skip; however, without the Environmental Scan and components of the Needs Assessment, jumping to this step may result in a misaligned improvement plan and lack of buy-in from key stakeholders.
- Final Report. The Final Report will share the findings of the Needs Assessment. It will include key data that supports the need to make changes, and findings that lead to the action steps and recommendations that have been identified. The Final Report should be used as both a roadmap on where to begin the work to make

changes and a tool to inform the broader constituency about the issues and the plan to make improvements.
- Implementation. Now, the implementation phase of the work begins, likely twelve to eighteen months after the initiation of this process. With large-scale change of this nature, it is important to identify an implementation timeline that is reasonable and does not create initiative overload.
- Evaluate. Throughout the implementation phase, ongoing evaluation of the impact of change should be monitored and reviewed. One should expect that with ongoing evaluation of impact, adjustments will be made to ensure maximum effectiveness.

Community Partner Spotlight: The JED Foundation

The Jed Foundation (JED) is a leading nonprofit that protects emotional health and prevents suicide for teens and young adults nationwide. They partner with high schools, districts, and colleges to strengthen their mental health, substance misuse, and suicide prevention programs and systems; equip teens and young adults with skills and knowledge to help themselves and each other; and encourage community awareness, understanding, and action for young adult mental health.

JED's work with schools is grounded in the Comprehensive Approach to Mental Health Promotion and Suicide Prevention. This evidence-based framework combines recommended practices and field expertise to help educational institutions create best-in-class mental health systems that foster connected, thriving school communities. With this approach, JED helps schools identify their strengths and needs to make meaningful and measurable improvements in student well-being. Today, JED impacts over 1,248 schools, districts, and campuses, reaching more than 6.5 million students from pre-K through college.

Building Support and Momentum

The Environmental Scan and Needs Assessment are critical actions to undertake to develop a comprehensive improvement plan. Equally important is the development of a plan to build support and momentum for the planned changes. Since the plan will likely include the redeployment of available resources, potentially making a decision to prioritize this work over other work important to the district, building support early is important. Building support early will help to prevent later pushback and disagreement about the direction of this work.

As you develop a change plan to improve student mental health support, there are two key considerations to help build support and momentum. You must develop a plan to build consensus around the urgency of the problem that needs to be addressed, as well as actively develop and carry out a communication plan. Both considerations are further discussed below.

Consensus Building

Like any change process, there will likely be individuals who are in deep support of the change, while others will question the necessity of any change. Often, while there are identified groups who stand on each side of the need to make change, there are many stakeholders who are disinterested or unaware of the issue. To support the necessary changes that will need to be made, you must engage in a deliberate consensus-building strategy and maximize the awareness of the importance of dealing with this.

The good news is that the activities associated with an Environmental Scan and Needs Assessment easily support early consensus building if done well. While it is possible to simply hire a consultant to come into your district to conduct an Environmental Scan and Needs Assessment, you would miss an opportunity to leverage these tasks in supporting consensus building. Taking on these tasks yourself or using a consultant to support the process, not take it over, will provide you with the opportunity to build consensus at the outset.

Launching the Steering Committee

As you initiate this work, it is recommended that you assemble a Steering Committee that will guide this process and engage in activities along the way that will support consensus building. The Steering Committee should broadly represent the many stakeholders within your community who support the improvement of services and support in the area of student mental health. Considerations of membership are those individuals who are committed to this work and/or represent a group that can support your work as you enter the implementation phase. It may also be helpful at this stage to consider inviting representation from groups or individuals who may be opposed to your plans.

A Steering Committee should be a broad representation of key stakeholders that are influential in the area that they represent. For example, for a district-wide effort, you should consider the following representation:

- School committee/board representative
- District-level representatives
- Building-based representatives
- School-based mental health representative
- Parent representatives
- Student representatives
- Community-based, local mental health representative
- School committee/board representative
- Local hospital representation
- City/town official representative
- Political (state representative or senator) representative
- District/town communications representative

Once established, the Steering Committee should meet on a regular schedule to support the work to improve mental health support for students. The Steering Committee will be actively engaged in either conducting or supporting a consultant to conduct the Environmental Scan and Needs Assessment. This group will also work to develop Action Plans as part of the Needs Assessment. Effective leadership of this group will lessen the workload on school staff.

Another key role of members of the Steering Committee is to regularly and proactively inform their circles about the work that is taking place along the way. As part of the planning of the role of Steering Committee members, ongoing communication with their sector should be an expected and planned occurrence. At the initiation of the Steering Committee, the development of specific roles of members should be articulated.

Responsibilities of membership should include an expectation that members exercise their influence to inform, answer questions, and build support for the improvement plan.

Developing a Communication Plan

Developing a Communication Plan at the outset of this work, and in parallel to the project plan, is essential for success. Without an intentional communication plan, you may run into opposition from internal and external stakeholders. Even with a well-developed and executed communication plan, you may run into opposition; however, an effective Communication Plan should support increased awareness and buy-in of your plan.

The change to support and services for student mental health will require both internal (within the district and schools) and external (broader community) changes to be successful. Developing an early and consistent Communication Plan will result in increased support as you move toward making change. The Communication Plan, developed with input from the Steering Committee, should provide expected activities and timelines to be accomplished. Here are a few of the key elements of the development of a Communication Plan.

- Define Goals. Your Communication Plan will have multiple goals that support the project. You should look to raise awareness and build support for change around the issue, share information about the components of the plan when developed, and share successes along the way.
- Identify Audiences. As part of the plan, you should identify the audiences and how you will meet their needs. This will likely include school/district staff, parent/guardian community, key decision-makers (e.g., school committee), and the broader community.
- Develop Talking Points. In planning, key talking points should be developed. You want to provide clear, accurate, and repeatable talking points to support message repetition and clarity. Some areas of talking points include why this is being undertaken, articulation of the scope of the problem, the imperative to make changes, and how this will benefit students academically.

- Communication Modalities. You will need to decide how you will get the message out. The use of multiple approaches will strengthen message penetration across stakeholder groups.
- Timeline and Phases. Develop a specific timeline around communication and the key messages that will be shared in each phase. The communication when you launch this work will evolve as you move from the Environmental Scan and Needs Assessment to implementing action and reviewing results.
- Plan to Gather Feedback. There will likely be feedback about the effectiveness, modality, and quality of the communication. Plan at the outset to provide opportunities to gather feedback on the communication strategy. This will allow for ongoing refinement of the plan.
- Plan for Flexibility. No developed plan is implemented exactly as developed. Plan to communicate adjustments and changes to the plan as you learn more and conditions change.
- Communicate Impact. At the outset, identify the metrics of success you will share with the community.

Developing a Communication Plan may be something that is atypical in practice. Often, the belief that schools and districts are doing the right things for kids is believed to be enough to garner the support for change. That is often not the case. Without a strong communication plan, the Steering Committee will become sidetracked by resistance to the Action Plan.

Community Partner Spotlight: kartoonEDU

In small-to-medium-sized school districts, having a dedicated role for district communications is a luxury, and having in-house visual media production is unheard of. When it comes to visual communications, most districts of this size get by with cellphone photography, screen capture, and slide presentations. Original production of video or animation is cost-prohibitive, spoils quickly, and requires a logistical commitment that is simply out of their realm.

kartoonEDU set out to solve each of these issues. Rather than focusing on the vibrant, gauzy, slow-motion video promotions that large districts may use for brand identity, school choice, or teacher recruitment, the Massachusetts-based startup uses animation and districts' unique visual identity to tackle the tough topics in education. By focusing on topics that are common to and not competitive between districts, kartoonEDU can create simple, digestible visual media for a district at a deeply discounted rate. It does this by using a fee-for-license structure to produce custom, one-of-a-kind media while reusing the non-proprietary, topical information other districts may also want to customize and license for their own use.

The result is durable, flexible, and affordable visual communications for districts of any size. Since its founding in 2023, kartoonEDU has worked with more than sixty districts, from Massachusetts to California, distilling difficult topics like budgets, school construction projects, anti-bullying, school safety, career and technical education, and Multi-Tiered Systems of Support (with the authors of this book). Moreover, because animation is so flexible, kartoonEDU has seamlessly reproduced topics in thirteen languages at just a fraction of the English-language license.

kartoonEDU serves this mission because it believes public education is the greatest vehicle for mobility in a well-functioning civil society. It dedicates its work to championing vital institutions while "turning down the temperature" on hot-button topics in a politically charged communications landscape.

Key Takeaways

- Taking the necessary time to understand the challenges and develop an Action Plan for change will support overall success.
- Leveraging a Steering Committee will provide multiple benefits to support the intended changes.
- Engaging in an Environmental Scan and Needs Assessment is a necessary starting point for plan development.
- Expect resistance to the planned change and pre-identify strategies to build support and momentum around the necessity of change.
- Develop a Communication Plan in parallel to an Action Plan.

What's Next?

In the next chapter, we'll explore how to fund and sustain a Tier 4 SEL program. We'll share ideas on how to gain access to seed funding and options for sustaining the program after this funding has expired.

9 SEL Tier 4 Components

In the previous chapter, we described the advantages of a Tier 4 model. This model offers the chance to deliver more direct and nuanced services to students. Integrating Tier 4 mental health supports into an MTSS system can significantly enhance student well-being. Such a system can address limitations in both a three-tiered MTSS and pediatric mental health outpatient systems.

The integration of Tier 4 supports, shown in Figure 9.1, such as proactive mental health screening, dedicated care coordination, in-school outpatient therapy, and wraparound mental health services, can lead to the following:

- Early detection of mental health concerns
- Serving a more significant number of students with diverse mental health and social service needs
- Reduced wait times for outpatient mental health services
- Better engagement of families to support students' mental health needs outside of school (see Figure 9.1)

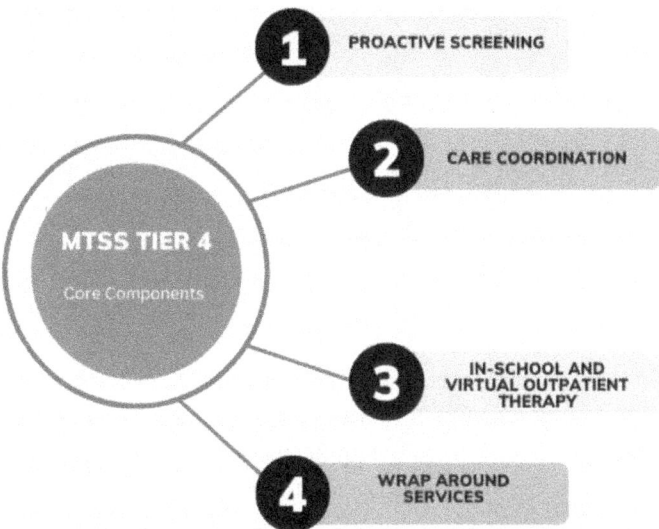

Figure 9.1 Components of a Tier 4 model.

In this chapter, we will explore each component and how to integrate them into a traditional MTSS system. Next, let's revisit the case of Oliver and consider how his treatment plan might differ from Tier 4 supports in his school.

> ## Revisiting the Case of Oliver
>
> As you will recall from the previous chapter, Oliver was a student dealing with undiagnosed anxiety that was impacting his social, emotional, and academic growth. Oliver attended a school with a traditional MTSS model, which took nearly an entire school year for Oliver's needs to be identified and supported. Now, let's imagine that Oliver instead attended a school with MTSS Tier 4 support. This will allow us to see, on a student level, the impact an MTSS Tier 4 program can have on social and emotional well-being and academic success.
>
> **September**
>
> Oliver is starting the first grade this year. Like his classmates, he is eager to meet his teacher and new classmates. Other than a few minor and typical miscues, Oliver sails through the first month of school. By all accounts, he appears to be making friends and can follow most classroom rules with only minor redirection.
>
> **October**
>
> Oliver has enjoyed the first six weeks of school. Along with all his classmates, he takes part in his school's universal screening program. His school uses the Pediatric System Checklist[1] to assess all K-2 students for social, emotional, and behavioral functioning. Oliver's screening results showed that he may have significant impairments in attention. Oliver's school adjustment counselor discusses the results with Oliver's mother, who agrees for Oliver to complete an additional assessment, the Screen for Child Anxiety Related Disorders (SCARED).[2] She also schedules an appointment with Oliver's pediatrician to have him evaluated for Attention Deficit Hyperactivity Disorder (ADHD).

November

As classroom expectations increase and social groups form, Oliver exhibits new behaviors. His teacher notices he is having difficulty sitting at his desk and frequently reminds him to return to his chair. His teacher must also often stop "circle time" on the rug to help Oliver calm down.

Oliver's SCARED assessment results indicate that there may be a presence of an anxiety disorder. Oliver's mother brings these screening results to his appointment with the pediatrician. At this appointment, Oliver's pediatrician screens him for ADHD. The results suggest that Oliver does not have ADHD. However, his pediatrician recommends that Oliver meet with a mental health clinician for an anxiety disorder evaluation.

Oliver's mother shares the information she's gathered from the pediatrician with his school adjustment counselor. She mentions that the pediatrician noted that it could be up to six months before Oliver is seen by a therapist due to insurance limitations. Oliver's school adjustment counselor suggests that he see a therapist as part of the school's in-school outpatient program. Oliver's mother agrees, and he begins to work with a therapist the following week.

December

Oliver has been working with a therapist for several weeks and has been formally diagnosed with generalized anxiety disorder. He is learning strategies for managing his anxiety, and his therapist has placed an internal referral for him to be evaluated by a psychiatrist within the therapist's practice. With a dual release in place, the therapist shares the strategies she and Oliver are working on with his school adjustment counselor, who then, with a parent release, shares this information with his teacher.

Oliver still has times when he struggles with self-regulation in class. During these moments, if necessary, his teacher and school adjustment counselor help him use the strategies he's learned in therapy. As a result, he rarely needs to leave the classroom as he can continue growing socially, emotionally, and academically.

January

Oliver continues with therapy and probably will for at least the next few months. His family helps support the strategies he's learned in therapy to manage his anxiety when at home and school. Oliver has been seen by a psychiatrist who does not recommend medication at this time, but they scheduled a follow-up appointment for June to check in on Oliver's symptoms.

June

Oliver had a very successful school year. With his anxiety managed, he was able to thrive both academically and socially. He is beyond grade level when it comes to reading and is at grade level in math. He has many friends and enjoys playing with them at recess and playground meet-ups on the weekends.

As you can see, Oliver's experience was much different at a school with an MTSS Tier 4 program. Oliver's case only highlights two of the four program components of an MTSS Tier 4 program. Still, it illustrates that schools don't need to fully implement all of the components to significantly impact student outcomes. That said, Oliver's success largely depended on the early identification of social and emotional needs made possible by universal screening. Since this MTSS Tier 4 program component is so critical, we'll begin a detailed examination of the MTSS Tier 4 program model with universal screening and identification practices.

Proactive Mental Health Screening and Identification Practices

As exemplified in the case of Oliver, proactively screening students for mental health concerns can drastically alter their trajectory socially, emotionally, and academically. Universal mental health screening in schools, regardless of apparent signs, can dramatically impact students' social, emotional, and academic paths. It involves proactively assessing all students' mental health and well-being. This approach offers several advantages:

- Early Detection and Intervention: Universal screening allows educators and mental health professionals to identify students who may be struggling with mental health challenges before these issues escalate.

Early detection enables early intervention and support, which can prevent more serious mental health problems from developing.
- Reduced Stigma: By implementing universal screening, schools can normalize conversations about mental health. It sends a message that mental health is as important as physical health, reducing the stigma associated with seeking help for mental health concerns. When everyone is screened, it becomes a routine part of maintaining overall well-being.
- Improved Academic Performance: Students with untreated mental health issues often struggle academically. By addressing these issues early, schools can provide appropriate support and accommodations, leading to improved academic performance. When students feel mentally well, they can better focus on their studies.
- Enhanced Student Well-Being: Universal mental health screening helps create a school environment that prioritizes the well-being of students. When students know their mental health is valued and supported, they are more likely to feel safe and connected, contributing to a positive school culture.
- Targeted Resources: Screening results can help schools allocate resources more effectively. By identifying specific mental health needs within the student population, schools can tailor their support programs and services to address those needs.
- Preventative Measures: Universal screening can identify students who may be at risk of developing mental health issues in the future. Schools can then implement preventative measures and provide education on coping strategies, resilience, and emotional regulation to help these students build mental resilience.
- Support for Families: Universal screening can be an opportunity to involve families in the mental health support process. When parents are aware of their child's mental health needs, they can collaborate with schools and mental health professionals to provide the necessary support at home.
- Data for Research and Policy: Aggregated data from universal screening can inform research and policymaking. It helps identify trends and patterns in student mental health, allowing schools and policymakers to make informed decisions about resource allocation and program development.

- Improved Long-Term Outcomes: Early intervention and support can positively impact a student's long-term mental health outcomes. Schools can help students develop the skills and resilience needed for a healthier adulthood by addressing mental health concerns during childhood and adolescence.
- Equity and Inclusivity: Universal screening ensures that all students have equal access to mental health support regardless of their background or circumstances. This promotes equity and inclusivity in education, as it does not rely on students or their families self-identifying mental health needs.

There are numerous ways to use universal screening to identify students who would benefit from mental health support. Before selecting which type(s) of screening is the best fit for your district or school, it is imperative to design a screening/identification strategy that meets your needs and aligns with your community's culture. We recommend considering your community culture surrounding mental health, the goals you hope to accomplish by proactively screening/identifying students needing mental health support, and your school/district's existing mental health support structures.

Before You Start

By considering your community's culture regarding student mental health, you'll likely land on an approach to mental health screening that will gain mass adoption. On the flip side, ignoring where your community stands on identifying and supporting students' mental health needs could lead to a disgruntled community that feels as though the school is overstepping its bounds. For instance, if your school is situated in a conservative community that has no or little experience with proactive, universal mental health screening, it would probably behoove you to start by using a strengths-based social and emotional learning competencies screener or by training educational staff to identify and refer students in need of mental health support.

However, suppose your community has experience with universal mental health screening and is more comfortable with proactive identification of student needs. In that case, you may be in a position to introduce universal screening that identifies student needs specific to generalized anxiety disorder or depression. Of course, even within the same community, comfort ranges will vary based on student age and development. In addition to considering community culture before moving to examine universal screening practices, it is also important to define the goals your school intends to accomplish by proactively screening/identifying students in need of mental health support.

The goals of proactive, universal mental health screening in schools seem obvious: identify students with mental health concerns and connect them with support. In some ways, this is true, but your district's individual circumstances make it important to clearly define your school's goals before creating a universal screening system. For instance, is your goal to identify population-based mental needs to inform your social and emotional learning Tier 1 instruction? Or do you intend to identify students with mental health needs who are not being supported through Tier 3 counseling to connect them to Tier 2 group counseling services?

It could also be that your school's goal is to identify students with moderate to severe mental health needs and refer them to community-based mental health services. Or it could be all of the above. Whatever your goal is, we recommend clearly defining it, as this will guide the creation of your approach to universal screening. Your approach will also be guided by the mental health support structures that are already in place.

The last thing you want to do is bury your head in the sand by avoiding proactive mental health screening because you are afraid of what you might find. However, it is wise to introduce a screening system that is aligned with your support structures. For example, if your school does not have a school social worker or adjustment counselor on staff, then you'll want to be sure to partner with a mental health agency to be onsite if you are screening for suicidality and depression.

Likewise, if your goal is to identify students for Tier 2 group counseling, you'll need to ensure that you have a school counselor available to deliver such support. The one caveat is that you may want to utilize universal screening to help justify additions to your school's social and emotional learning curriculum. For instance, by screening students for social and emotional learning competencies, you may discover that 64 percent of students display large areas for growth in self-regulation.

This information may help justify a Tier 1 social and emotional learning program that teaches mindfulness techniques. Once you have considered your school's current mental health support structures, defined the goals connected to universal screening, and have gained an understanding of your community's culture around mental health, then you are ready to design and implement a proactive, universal mental health screening system.

Approaches to Universal Mental Health Screening

Once you have defined the goals of your universal mental health screening system, understand what type of screening fits best in your community, and plan how to assist students who need support, you can decide which type(s) of screening to implement. The most used universal mental health screening models are some combination of social and emotional learning competency screening, social, emotional, and behavioral functioning screening, and screening for mental health disorders (anxiety, depression, and suicidality).

Social and Emotional Learning Competency Screening

Social and Emotional Learning (SEL) Competency Screening is used to assess and evaluate a student's social and emotional skills and competencies. These competencies encompass a range of interpersonal and intrapersonal abilities crucial for effective communication, relationship building, and emotional well-being. Most commonly assessed are the core SEL competencies defined by The Collaborative for Academic, Social, and Emotional Learning (CASEL): self-awareness, self-management, social awareness, relationship skills, and responsible decision-making. SEL competency screening often utilizes standardized assessment tools or questionnaires designed to measure various aspects of social and emotional skills.

These tools may include self-report surveys, teacher or parent evaluations, or direct observations. This data can be collected solely from the student or from multiple sources.

Depending on the student's age, a school may want to collect data from teachers, parents, or caregivers to gain a comprehensive understanding of an individual's social and emotional strengths and areas for improvement. The collected data is analyzed objectively to assess an individual's social and emotional competency level. This evaluation helps identify areas where intervention or support may be needed for individuals and populations of students.

Based on the screening results, educators, counselors, or mental health professionals can develop personalized interventions and strategies to enhance a student's social and emotional skills. These interventions may include targeted classroom activities, counseling, or group therapy sessions. Universal SEL competency screening may also be used to identify students who could benefit from more targeted screening like mental health disorder screening or social, emotional, and behavioral functioning screening, which we'll discuss next.

Social, Emotional, and Behavioral Functioning Screening

Social, Emotional, and Behavioral Functioning Screening (SEBFS) in schools is a systematic process used to assess and evaluate students' overall well-being, including their social, emotional, and behavioral development. This screening approach is designed to identify students who may be facing challenges in these areas and require additional support or intervention. The primary objective of SEBFS is to identify students who may be experiencing difficulties in social interactions, managing their emotions, or displaying challenging behaviors.

This can encompass a wide range of issues, such as anxiety, depression, aggression, or social isolation. SEBFS is often used as a detection mechanism to identify potential concerns at an early stage. Early identification, through the use of a standardized assessment tool, allows for timely interventions and support, which can help prevent more severe problems from developing.

SEBFS typically employs various assessment tools and instruments to gather information about a student's social, emotional, and behavioral functioning. These tools most often include standardized questionnaires that can be completed by students, teachers, or parents, depending on the tool used and the student's developmental stage. Based on the screening results, schools can develop individualized support plans for students needing additional help. These plans may include counseling, social skills training, behavior modification strategies, or referrals to mental health professionals.

While SEBFS is important for identifying and addressing problems, schools also use it as a tool for promoting positive social and emotional development. It can be used to identify areas where social and emotional learning programs and initiatives can be beneficial for all students. Like SEL competency screening, SEBFS screening is most often used to screen entire school populations, while screening for mental health disorders is often best used for screening specific grade levels or as a follow-up screen for students who have been identified as needing additional support through a universal screening process.

Mental Health Disorder Screening

Mental health disorder screening in schools is a systematic process used to identify students who may be experiencing or are at risk of developing mental health disorders. This screening is designed to assess students' emotional well-being, psychological functioning, and the presence of any signs or symptoms that may indicate the need for further evaluation and support. By identifying potential mental health concerns in students at an early stage, educators and support staff can intervene promptly to provide appropriate assistance and prevent more severe problems from developing.

The screening process aims to identify a range of mental health concerns, such as anxiety disorders, depression, eating disorders, attention deficit hyperactivity disorder (ADHD), substance abuse, self-harm, or suicidal ideation. The data collected through mental health disorder screening is evaluated objectively to assess the severity and nature of the student's mental health concerns. This assessment informs decisions regarding further evaluation, intervention, or referral to mental health professionals.

When students are identified as potentially needing help, schools should have procedures in place to refer them to appropriate mental health services or professionals. Additionally, schools may offer in-school counseling or support groups to address specific mental health needs. Unlike SEL or SEBFS, mental health disorder screening is often a precursor to a child being diagnosed with a mental health concern that requires treatment. Due to this distinction, we recommend using this screening modality for specific target populations.

Using mental health disorder screening for targeted populations could take many forms. For instance, your school may want to screen entire grades that are more susceptible to mental health concerns. The onset of adolescent depression can occur at various ages, but it is most commonly observed to emerge during early to mid-adolescence. Typically, the highest risk period for the onset of depression in adolescents is between the ages of twelve and eighteen, with many cases becoming noticeable around fifteen to sixteen years old. Therefore, your school may consider screening all tenth-grade students annually for depression and suicidality.

Similarly, adolescents with low self-efficacy, which is the belief in their ability to handle challenging situations and achieve goals effectively, may be more prone to anxiety. When they doubt their capabilities, they may experience heightened anxiety when faced with academic, social, or personal challenges. As a result, if you have conducted universal SEL screening, which includes assessing students' self-efficacy, you may consider using a generalized anxiety screener only with students who scored low in self-efficacy. In addition to the three universal screening modalities we've shared, schools can support "gatekeeper training" to help staff better identify students with mental health concerns.

Gatekeeper Training

Gatekeeper training refers to a specialized education program designed to train individuals in recognizing the signs of mental health issues, suicidal ideation, or crises and equipping them with the skills and knowledge to provide initial assistance or refer individuals to appropriate professional help. The term "gatekeeper" refers to someone who stands at the metaphorical gate and can help identify and guide individuals toward appropriate mental health resources and support. Gatekeepers are typically people in various roles who are likely to encounter individuals at risk of mental health challenges, such as teachers, school counselors, and other K-12 school staff.

Gatekeeper training teaches participants to recognize the warning signs and risk factors associated with mental health issues and suicidal thoughts. This may involve understanding behavioral changes, mood shifts, and verbal cues that suggest distress.

Gatekeepers are trained to assess the level of risk and the severity of a person's mental health crisis or suicidal ideation. This helps in determining the appropriate level of intervention and support needed. Participants learn how to communicate empathetically and nonjudgmentally with individuals in distress. Effective listening and communication skills are crucial for creating a supportive and safe environment. Gatekeepers are instructed on connecting individuals in crisis to appropriate mental health professionals, services, or resources. They are not expected to provide therapy or treatment themselves but to facilitate access to professional care.

In a paper published by the American Council on Education (ACE), titled "What Works for Improving Mental Health in Higher Education?," it was shared that gatekeeper training has demonstrated questionable effectiveness. As a result, to increase effectiveness, ACE recommends a "saturation approach" to gatekeeper training, in which all faculty and staff receive training and brief training boosters. Although this recommendation was for places of higher education, this recommendation feels applicable to K-12 schools as well. In the coming section, we'll discuss how to design an effective approach to gatekeeper training and how to select a universal screening tool.

Selecting a Universal Screening Tool or Gatekeeper Training

Selecting a universal mental health screening questionnaire for use in a school is an important decision that requires careful consideration. Whenever possible, the choice of a universal mental health screening questionnaire should be a collaborative effort involving educators, mental health professionals, parents, and students to ensure it meets your school community's specific needs and goals. Here are some key factors to take into account when selecting a universal mental health screening tool:

Purpose and Goals

- Define the purpose of the screening. Is it for early identification, monitoring student well-being, or identifying population-based needs to guide Tier-1 programming?
- Clearly outline the goals and objectives you aim to achieve through the screening process.

Validity and Reliability

- Ensure that the questionnaire has been validated for use in the school-age population.

- Verify that the instrument is reliable, meaning it consistently measures what it's intended to measure.

Age and Developmental Appropriateness

- Consider the age group of the students who will be taking the questionnaire. It should be age-appropriate and sensitive to developmental differences.
- Consider whether or not students of all age groups can access the screening tool or if teachers and parents will be completing the screener instead.

Cultural Sensitivity

- Ensure that the questionnaire is culturally sensitive and appropriate for your students' diverse backgrounds and identities.
- It should avoid bias and be available in multiple languages if necessary.

Ease of Administration and Analysis

- Evaluate the ease of administering the questionnaire. It should be user-friendly for both students and school staff.
- The length of the questionnaire should be considered. Universal screening should be conducted several times a year. This becomes challenging when students and teachers are asked to complete lengthy questionnaires.
- Consider the time and resources required to administer and score the questionnaire. It should be feasible within the school's schedule and staffing constraints.

Scoring and Interpretation

- Determine how the questionnaire is scored and interpreted. Are there clear guidelines for identifying students who may need further evaluation or support?

Table 9.1 Screening Tools

Screening Category	Recommended Screening Tools
Social and Emotional Learning Competencies Screening	Panorama Education, Devereux Strengths Assessment (DESSA), Devereux Strengths Assessment Mini, Social Emotional Assets and Resilience Scales (SEARS), Satchel Pulse
Social, Emotional, and Behavioral Functioning Screening	Behavioral and Emotional Screening System (BESS), Social Skills Improvement System (SSIS), Behavior Intervention Monitoring Assessment System (BIMAS), Pediatric Symptom Checklist (PSC)
Mental Health Disorder Screening	Patient Health Questionnaire (PHQ-9), Generalized Anxiety Disorder Scale (GAD-7), Brief Screen for Adolescent Depression (BSAD), Screen for Child Anxiety Related Disorders (SCARED)

Cost

- Is the cost of the questionnaire applied at a per-pupil rate for unlimited administration? Or is there a cost associated with each administration?
- If the tool does not have the cost of analysis built in, what resources will need to be dedicated to analyzing and sharing student results?

Once you create a set of criteria for the universal screening tool you would like to use in your school, it is time to select a screening tool. The table above is a list of screening tools that we believe to be worthy of your consideration (Table 9.1).

Selecting an Approach to Gatekeeper Training

Selecting a gatekeeper training program for use in a school is an important step in promoting mental health awareness, treatment, and suicide prevention. Here are key considerations when choosing a gatekeeper training program:

Evidence-Based Content

- Ensure that the training program is evidence-based, meaning it is grounded in research and has demonstrated effectiveness in equipping gatekeepers to recognize signs of distress and take appropriate action.

Training Goals and Objectives

- Define clear goals and learning objectives for the training program, such as increasing knowledge, improving skills, and changing attitudes related to mental health and suicide prevention.
- Assess whether the training program addresses the specific mental health challenges and prevalent risk factors in your school or community.

Cultural Sensitivity and Diversity

- Ensure that the training content is culturally inclusive of diverse populations by identifying mental health disparities and cultural differences regarding mental health stigma and treatment.

Training Format, Duration, and Frequency

- Consider the training format, whether in-person, online, or a combination of both. Choose a format that is accessible and convenient for the target audience.
- Determine the length of the training sessions and the frequency for ongoing training or refresher courses.

Cost and Budget

- Assess the cost of the training program and ensure it aligns with your school's budget for mental health initiatives.
- Consider the long-term sustainability of the training program, including plans for ongoing training and support.

After you've identified the type of training, budget, and sustainability plan, it is time to select the training that works best for your school. The Table 9.2 is a list of gatekeeper training options that we recommend considering:

Table 9.2 Gatekeeper Training

Training Name	Description
Question, Persuade, Refer	QPR is a widely recognized gatekeeper training program that teaches participants how to recognize signs of suicide risk, ask direct questions, persuade individuals to seek help and make referrals to appropriate resources.
Youth Mental Health First Aid	MHFA provides training to adults who work with or support young people. It covers a range of mental health issues and teaches participants how to provide initial assistance to a young person experiencing a mental health crisis.
Boston University Mental Health Learning Module for Educators	BU offers two modules for elementary and secondary educators that aim to help school staff identify and refer students with mental health concerns. These twenty-minute modules are open source and can be customized by districts.
Safe TALK	Safe TALK is a half-day training program that aims to increase awareness of suicide risk and teach participants how to recognize signs, engage with individuals at risk, and connect them to appropriate resources.
Signs of Suicide	SOS is a school-based program that combines suicide prevention education with screening. It includes a curriculum for students and training for school staff.
Kognito	Kognito offers a range of online simulations and role-playing programs for educators, students, and other school staff to practice responding to individuals in distress. Their programs cover topics such as mental health, suicide prevention, and substance abuse.
Erika's Lighthouse	Erika's Lighthouse provides online mental health education programs for schools, including gatekeeper training to increase awareness and promote early intervention.

An ideal Tier 4 system will combine the use of universal mental health screening and gatekeeper training. Combining these modalities helps to proactively identify students who are in need of mental health support. Once identified, schools should help to facilitate mental health treatment. One of the ways schools can do this is to support mental health care coordination.

Dedicated Care Coordination

The Need for Care Coordination?

Finding a pediatric mental health care provider can be a complex and challenging process due to various factors such as the following:

- Limited Availability: There is often a shortage of mental health care providers, especially in certain regions and specific specialties. This shortage can result in long wait times and limited options for individuals seeking care.
- Insurance Coverage: Navigating insurance coverage for mental health services can be confusing. Some providers may not accept certain insurance plans, leaving patients to pay out-of-pocket or seek in-network providers. Insurance companies may also have limitations on the number of sessions or types of services covered.
- Matching Needs: Finding a provider specializing in a particular mental health condition or therapy type can be challenging. Individuals may need to search extensively to find a provider that meets their needs and preferences.
- Geographic Location: Location can be a significant factor. Rural areas often have fewer mental health providers, making it difficult for individuals in these areas to access care. Transportation issues can also be a barrier to attending appointments.
- Long Wait Times: Even when individuals find a suitable provider, they may face long wait times for initial assessments and ongoing treatment. This delay can exacerbate mental health issues and deter some from seeking help altogether.
- Provider-Patient Compatibility: The relationship between a mental health provider and their patient is crucial for successful treatment. Finding a provider with whom one feels comfortable and can establish a therapeutic rapport can be a time-consuming process.

Finding specialized mental health care for children and adolescents can be especially complex, as providers must have expertise in pediatric mental health and be equipped to work with young individuals and their families. However, by integrating dedicated care coordination into an MTSS Tier 4 model, schools can help greatly improve the process of finding outpatient mental health services for families and their students.

Defining Care Coordination

Mental health care coordination services aim to optimize the care provided to individuals dealing with mental health challenges by matching them with a clinician that best meets their needs. Mental health care coordination services should be staffed by trained professionals who can help patrons navigate the complex and challenging process of accessing pediatric mental health services. The two predominant models of mental health care coordination are the hotline model and the onsite model.

Onsite model: With the onsite model, a school hires and trains a professional to coordinate care for students and families. The Care Coordinator would field calls from families and school counselors seeking outpatient mental health services for students. The Care Coordinator would triage the referral, ensuring that they don't need emergency services, and then work to match the student with an outpatient mental health provider that meets their needs. In this model, the Care Coordinator can build ongoing relationships with callers and local mental health care providers. However, the school must dedicate resources to providing a salary, benefits, and space to support this type of position.

Hotline model: This model is similar to the onsite model, as hotlines are staffed by trained professionals who can triage callers, refer them to emergency services, or proceed with helping to match them with outpatient mental health care services. Care coordination hotlines are generally accessible via phone, text, or online messaging. In this model, schools partner with hotline care coordination service providers. This allows schools to avoid the overhead of hiring a dedicated staff member to provide this service. Still, on the other hand, the caller or local providers can't build a relationship with the care coordinator when adopting the hotline model.

Benefits of Care Coordination

Students and Families

There are several benefits associated with instituting dedicated mental health care coordination. Families and students directly using the service gain the most from care coordination, but school counselors and, in turn, all students benefit from their school adopting a dedicated mental health care coordination service.

Families and students who use the care coordination service to gain access to outpatient mental health services can expect to save time and experience less stress. When a parent or guardian accesses care coordination services, they are likely to learn about the types of mental health providers, therapies, and interventions that may suit their child's needs. Many care coordination services will conduct an initial triage and assessment of the student's needs to understand the urgency and level of care needed.

Next, the care coordinator will gain an understanding of the caller's insurance coverage, geographic, demographic, language, and clinical preferences. The mental health care coordination will then help to schedule an appointment with a mental health provider, ensuring timely access to care. Care coordinators often conduct follow-up calls or check-ins to monitor individuals' progress and ensure they receive the care they need. This "one-stop-shop" approach to coordinated mental health care services relieves families and students of an enormous burden. It also has a tremendous impact on school counselors.

School Counselors

Dedicated mental health care coordination for students can benefit school counselors, ultimately enhancing their ability to support students' well-being. Here are some ways in which this approach can be advantageous:

- Expertise and Specialization: Mental health care coordinators often have specialized training and experience in mental health issues and navigating the mental health care system. This expertise can complement the skills and knowledge of school counselors, who may have a broader range of responsibilities.
- Reduced Workload: School counselors typically have heavy caseloads, and adding the responsibility of coordinating mental health care for students can be overwhelming. Outsourcing this task can alleviate some of their workload, allowing them to focus more on direct counseling services and academic support.
- Access to Resources: Mental health care coordinators can connect students and families with a wider range of resources and services that may be beyond the knowledge base of a school counselor. They can help students access therapists, support groups, and other mental health services that may not be readily available through the school or within the school's geographic location.

- Improved Efficiency: Coordinators can streamline the process of getting students the help they need by handling administrative tasks, such as scheduling appointments and managing paperwork. This allows counselors to spend more time providing counseling and support.
- Better Continuity of Care: Dedicated coordinators can help ensure that students receive continuous care, even when transitioning between different schools, providers, or services. This can be particularly important for students with complex mental health needs.
- Focus on Prevention: With the administrative burden of care coordination off their shoulders, school counselors can invest more time in Tier 1 and Tier 2 preventive measures, such as developing and implementing mental health education programs, promoting mental health awareness, and identifying early signs of mental health issues.
- Reduced Burnout: By utilizing dedicated mental health care coordination services, school counselors can potentially reduce their stress levels and mitigate burnout, allowing them to remain effective and dedicated to their students over the long-term.

Integrating dedicated mental health care coordination into a Tier 4 program can help to improve student access to outpatient services and can greatly reduce the amount of time school counselors spend trying to match students with providers. The benefits associated with dedicated mental health care coordination are multiplied greatly when paired with an in-school outpatient therapy program.

Community Partner Spotlight: Care Solace

Care Solace is a mental health care coordination service and a school-based electronic health record system developer. Care Solace supports K-12 schools by connecting their students, families, and counselors to find mental health treatment providers and by streamlining the reimbursement process by allowing school mental health providers to bill for their services through the use of an electronic health record. By utilizing these two services, school systems are able to increase student access to mental health care and support school counselors in spending more time working directly with students.

Through Care Solace's vast network of providers, they can match students, their families, and school employees with mental health clinicians based on their needs, insurance, and preferences. In a discussion with Chad Castruita, Care Solace's Founder and CEO, he noted that "when a person logs on to their health insurance portal and are provided with a list of clinicians, often up to 40% of that list of providers is inaccurate."

Often, the provider no longer accepts that insurance or is not currently accepting new patients. As you can imagine, this results in parents, caregivers, and school counselors wasting a great deal of their time trying to locate providers for students and leaves them feeling frustrated and distraught. Care Solace seeks to remedy this issue by bringing clarity to the process and by lifting the burden of identifying providers from parents, caregivers, and school counselors.

As a result of their system, users can gain access to mental health providers covered by their insurance and that meet their preferences in a timely manner. In addition to streamlining student mental health care coordination, Care Solace is also working to make student mental health services provided by school staff sustainable and efficient through the development of an electronic health record.

Throughout the United States, school-based mental health clinicians can be reimbursed for services they provide to students insured by Medicaid. However, these reimbursement funds are often dispersed at the municipal or county level and never reach the school. In states like California, legislation is being proposed that would allow schools to seek reimbursement payments directly from insurance companies, both public and private.

This model would help to create a self-sustaining school-mental health workforce and increase access to support for students. But to make this a viable option for schools, they'll need a system that will allow them to document and bill for their services. Care Solace has created an electronic health record system for schools that is designed to obtain students' insurance information and consent, as well as translate clinical activities into insurance codes.

Care Solace is playing a pivotal role in transforming the landscape of student mental health support by addressing the challenges of provider access, administrative inefficiency, and reimbursement. By offering a robust network of vetted providers and an innovative electronic health record system, Care Solace ensures that students receive timely, quality care while alleviating the burden on parents, caregivers, and school staff.

The integration of insurance verification and billing capabilities into the platform not only enhances the sustainability of school-based mental health services but also fosters a more efficient and equitable system for students and families. As legislative changes continue to evolve, Care Solace's model stands poised to create lasting, positive impacts on mental health care access within schools, ensuring that all students have the support they need to thrive academically and emotionally.

In-School Outpatient Therapy

An in-school outpatient therapy program is a specialized mental health service provided within a school setting to support students who are in need of outpatient mental health services. Typically, one or more licensed outpatient therapists are embedded within a school setting to provide outpatient care during the school day. These therapists are not school employees but rather outpatient providers who are practicing within a school setting. This status allows the providers to continue typical outpatient practices, such as billing insurance while working within a school. Many benefits are associated with an in-school outpatient therapy program for students, families, and providers.

Benefits

Increased Access: The prevalence of pediatric mental health concerns has caused a bottleneck for students seeking outpatient services during after-school or weekend hours. Meanwhile, most clinicians who support school-aged children have empty offices while students are in school. By opening up the opportunity for students to engage in therapy during the school day, access to care is significantly increased. Additionally, the provider benefits by filling their daytime hours or being able to shift their workweek hours to free up more time for themselves in the evenings or on weekends.

Ideal location: These programs are typically located within the school premises, making them easily accessible to students. This proximity reduces barriers to access and helps integrate mental health support into the students' daily routines. Additionally, by locating therapeutic services in school, major barriers such as transportation are eliminated, allowing students to attend therapy more consistently. This consistency has been shown to improve outcomes for patients. Also, this benefits the therapists as well, who have a lower risk of patient "no-shows," which result in a loss of income for the provider.

Enhanced Collaboration with School Personnel: Therapists often collaborate closely with teachers, school counselors, and other staff members to address the student's emotional and behavioral challenges when embedded within the school environment. This coordination helps create a supportive and consistent approach.

Cost efficiency: In-school outpatient therapy programs can be cost-effective compared to the school providing internal mental health services. In essence, the cost of these programs can be free to schools, besides supplying the outpatient provider with space within a school building. This is a large financial saving compared to hiring a school adjustment counselor or social worker to provide therapeutic services for students. Additionally, this is a cost-effective model for providers, as they can often bill for up to six individual sessions per school day when their offices would otherwise be empty.

In-school outpatient therapy programs aim to create a safe and supportive environment within the school, helping students address their mental health challenges while minimizing disruptions to their education. These programs can play a crucial role in promoting the overall well-being of students and fostering their academic success. Still, a school must find willing and effective outpatient therapists to partner with in this work.

Identifying Partners

In-school outpatient therapy programs must be staffed by licensed and trained mental health professionals, such as clinical social workers, psychologists, or counselors. These professionals also must have expertise in working with children and adolescents. Ideally, it's best to pair outpatient therapists interested in working with a particular age group with the appropriate school. For instance, a therapist might love working with middle school students but has little interest in working with early elementary school-aged children. Also, schools should identify therapists who accept insurance that matches their students' needs.

Often, larger mental health groups are the providers that accept public health insurance. At the same time, independent therapists or smaller provider groups may be more likely to accept commercial insurance. In an ideal world, an in-school outpatient therapy program would collaborate with a mix of providers that accept both public and commercial insurance. This approach ensures that students, regardless of their insurance, can access providers within a school's program. In addition to making sure insurance needs match both the provider and student population, it is important to consider the provider's perceived benefits of entering into such a partnership.

With the advent of telehealth and the increase in pediatric mental health concerns, there is little motivation for clinicians to work within an in-school outpatient mental health setting. Therefore, it is critical to identify therapists who perceive the benefit of this type of partnership. For example, finding a provider that is eager to be home during after-school hours, maybe they have school-aged children, or on the weekends might have a desire to work within this type of partnership. You may also identify providers who truly enjoy being in a school setting and the collaboration with school counselors that comes with an in-school outpatient therapy program. If you don't have access to office space for a provider or do not have local clinicians interested in providing therapy on school grounds, you may want to consider telehealth therapy.

Teletherapy

Teletherapy, also known as online therapy or telehealth therapy, is a form of mental health counseling or therapy conducted remotely through technology. Instead of meeting with a therapist in person, a student would meet virtually with their therapist during the school day. Although this approach is likely appealing to therapists, it is important to consider the issues of safety, privacy, and age effectiveness when considering teletherapy in school settings.

When conducting teletherapy sessions at school, many potential risks exist. The first and most important is that of student safety. If teletherapy is going to be offered in school, it is critical to develop clear protocols for assessing students' mental health risks during teletherapy sessions. Establish procedures for handling emergencies, such as suicidal ideation or threats of harm, and ensure therapists know how to respond appropriately and quickly.

Additionally, a school must ensure student privacy by using secure teletherapy platforms and technologies that protect the privacy and confidentiality of students' personal and health information. These platforms must comply with relevant data privacy laws, such as the Health Insurance Portability and Accountability Act (HIPAA). It is our recommendation that any school considering adopting an in-school teletherapy model consult with legal counsel experienced in education and healthcare law to ensure that your school's teletherapy program complies with all relevant regulations and legal requirements.

We also recommend considering the clinical effectiveness of teletherapy access for developmental ages before moving forward with an in-school teletherapy program.

Teletherapy can be effective for individuals of various age groups, but its appropriateness and effectiveness can vary depending on the age and developmental stage of the person receiving therapy. Please refer to Table 9.3 for considerations for different age groups.

Ultimately, the effectiveness of teletherapy depends on the individual's comfort with technology, the nature of their mental health concerns, and

Table 9.3 Teletherapy Recommendations

Age Range	Considerations
5 and under	Not recommended for this age group.
6–12	• Teletherapy can be effective for children in this age group, but it often requires the involvement of parents or guardians who can assist with technology setup and facilitate sessions. • Some children may have shorter attention spans, so sessions may need to be shorter and more interactive.
13–18	• Teletherapy is generally well-suited for adolescents. Many teenagers are comfortable with technology and may be more open to engaging in virtual therapy sessions. • Adolescents may appreciate the privacy and convenience of teletherapy, as it allows them to receive counseling without needing transportation or face-to-face meetings.

their willingness to engage in therapy through digital means. Teletherapy providers often conduct assessments to determine if online therapy is a suitable option for potential clients and may recommend in-person services if necessary. Although adding an in-school outpatient therapy program can greatly increase access and the effectiveness of care, its reach is limited by the time and geography of the school building. However, including a wraparound mental health services program in a school's MTSS Tier 4 program adds additional care for students and families.

Wraparound Mental Health Services

Model Components

A wraparound service mental health model is a comprehensive and holistic approach to providing care and support for individuals with mental health needs, particularly those with complex or severe mental health conditions. This model aims to "wrap" a range of services and supports around the individual and their family to address their unique needs. Wraparound mental health programs can vary by function and form. Often recognized as the "gold standard" for providing mental health wraparound services for children and adolescents is the Children's Behavioral Health Initiative, more commonly known as the CBHI model.

The CBHI model, which should be staffed by at least one independently licensed mental health clinician, breaks down wraparound services into several subcategories, which include intensive care coordination, in-home therapy, family support and training, therapeutic mentoring services, parent mentoring, and in-home behavioral health services. Intensive care coordination is a staple of the CBHI model.

Acting as a care coordinator, a wraparound service specialist will bring all parties involved in the student's mental health care plan around the table to work toward a common goal. Often, these parties will include outpatient therapists, social workers, school counselors, teachers, parents/guardians, and other relatives. Together, this often fragmented team will work to help ensure that the student reaches their mental health goals.

Although not typically found within the traditional CBHI approach, the Wraparound Service Specialist will also help to coordinate ancillary social services that are not in direct service to a student's mental health but can certainly have a positive impact on their mental well-being. These services include but are not limited to housing assistance, food services (food pantries and supplemental nutrition assistance), and fuel assistance. Another primary component of the CBHI model is in-home therapy.

In-home therapy allows a wraparound specialist to work with the whole family, not just the child. The therapy sessions take place in the home and community to help the child and family resolve conflicts, learn new ways to talk to and understand each other, create new helpful routines, and find community resources. In addition to providing intensive care coordination and in-home therapy, a wraparound specialist will work within the CBHI model to coordinate other services, such as family support and training, therapeutic mentoring services, and in-home behavioral health services.

A wraparound specialist is able to help coordinate family support and training that can be provided by Family Partners. Family Partners are parents or caregivers of children with special needs who understand what families go through and can share their experiences. Although they will not be providing mental health services, they can provide coaching to families so that they can work to meet their child's mental health needs. A similar type of service provided within the CBHI model is therapeutic mentoring.

Many students who are challenged by mental health concerns want to get along with others but need help learning how to connect with people. A wraparound specialist can help connect students with a therapeutic mentor who can teach them social and communication skills and help the student practice these skills in everyday settings. Like a therapeutic mentor, an in-home behavioral health team will support students by working with them in real-life settings.

A wraparound specialist can support families who have students who are having a difficult time changing their behavior as a result of a mental health concern by coordinating in-home behavioral services. An in-home behavioral team will work with students to create a behavior plan that will help them change these challenging behaviors to improve their mental health and their daily lives. This intensive in-home and community-based approach to supporting student mental health is not traditionally part of the MTSS system but can provide significant benefits to students and their families.

Benefits

The integration of a wraparound mental health program within an MTSS Tier 4 model provides numerous benefits to the student, their families, and the school. Many of these benefits are gained through the ability for the wraparound clinician to literally meet the families where they are, which is in their homes. Eliminating the barriers associated with a traditional school-based mental health model, such as time, travel, and stigma, can make a significant difference in family engagement and, as a result, improve outcomes for students.

The traditional in-school mental health model requires families to engage with school teams on school grounds during school hours. This approach is convenient for school-based personnel but does not consider that this is not always a model that families are able or willing to engage in. There are many barriers associated with family engagement in the traditional school-based mental health model, and here are some of the most common:

- Work Constraints: Many families have demanding work schedules that make it challenging to attend school events or meetings during school hours. Some may not have the flexibility to take time off work.
- Transportation Issues: Families who don't have access to reliable transportation may find it difficult to come to the school, especially if it's not within walking distance. This is particularly relevant in areas with limited public transportation.
- Language Barriers: Families who are not fluent in the language used at the school may feel uncomfortable attending meetings or events where communication could be a barrier.
- Previous Negative Experiences: Families who have had negative or unpleasant experiences with school staff or other parents in the past may be hesitant to engage with the school again.
- Personal Challenges: Families dealing with personal challenges such as mental health issues, addiction, or family crises may find it difficult to engage with the school.
- Fear of Judgment: Families who feel judged or criticized by counselors, teachers, administrators, or other families may avoid school involvement to avoid further scrutiny.

Offering a wraparound mental health model that is flexible to meet families in their homes or within the community during non-school hours can help mitigate these barriers. This shift in approach can go a long way toward enhancing the relationship and levels of trust between the school and families. By establishing a trusting relationship, families are more likely to engage in one of the most pivotal benefits of a wraparound mental health program: in-home therapy.

In-home family therapy can offer several advantages for families and schools in supporting various student mental health issues and challenges. First, the in-home therapy approach provides families with a comfortable environment. Engaging in family therapy within the home often helps everyone involved feel more relaxed and open, which can lead to more productive and honest discussions. Second, it allows the wraparound therapist to observe family interactions in their natural environment, gaining valuable insights into family dynamics, communication patterns, and relationships. This helps therapists tailor interventions more effectively.

Once gaining this insight, the therapist can help families immediately apply the skills and strategies learned in therapy to their everyday lives since they practice them in their home setting. These skills and strategies learned in the home environment are more likely to be sustained over the long-term because they are practiced in the setting where they are needed most. Finally, the therapist can support families in their time of greatest need. For instance, if a family is having difficulty helping their student get to school in the morning, the therapist can be present to observe the morning routine and offer precise recommendations to best support the student and their family. In addition to the wraparound mental health model providing these important benefits to the student and family, it is also an appealing model to the clinician.

As described above, the wraparound model offers many benefits to the clinician's practice. Having the ability to observe and provide therapeutic interventions within the home improves patient outcomes, which in turn enhances the job satisfaction of the clinician. Also, increasing job satisfaction is the schedule and salary structure associated with an in-school wraparound mental health model.

A clinician contemplating whether or not to apply for a school-based wraparound specialist position would certainly be drawn to the potential to have the summer months off of work and to be freed from the fee-for-service model that most clinicians operate within. We'll dive deeper into what type of medical billing wraparound specialists can use to support their own salary in the next chapter. Still, before examining those specifics, a school should consider which wraparound model is the best fit for its community.

School-Based Wraparound Mental Health Models

Integrating a school-based wraparound health model into an MTSS Tier 4 model adds a critical dimension to student and family support. There are several ways to implement a wraparound program. In Table 9.4, you'll find three potential models for schools to use as a starting point:

Each school must decide which model most fits their community's needs. They must also consider what funding sources are available to start a wraparound program.

Table 9.4 Wraparound Program Models

Recommended Staff	Program Design
Master's level wraparound specialist	A clinician works independently to provide all of the program offerings (in-home therapy, therapeutic mentoring, and care coordination) while not diving deeply into any one arm of the program.
Independently licensed master's level wraparound specialist + bachelor's level therapeutic mentor	The master's level clinician supervises the bachelor's level team member who provides therapeutic mentoring after school hours and completes much of the care coordination. The wraparound specialist focuses most of their time on in-home therapy and building community connections.
Independently licensed master's level wraparound specialist + bachelor's level therapeutic mentor + bachelor's level family partner	The master's level wraparound specialist provides supervision to both the therapeutic mentor and the family partner. The family partner provides coaching to parents and caregivers so that they can effectively support their child's mental health needs. The addition of the family partner frees the WrapAround Specialist to spend more time providing clinical internvetions and coordinating community supports.
Independently licensed master's level wraparound specialist + bachelor's level therapeutic mentor + famly partner + master's level therapist	The master's level wraparound specialist provides supervision to the therapeutic mentor, family partner and the Master's level therapist. The Master's level therapist focuses solely on providing in-home therapy to the students with the greatest level of need. In addition to providing clinician supervision, the wraparound specialist spends much of their time in the community building connections with providers and youth-serving agencies.

Key Takeaways

- The MTSS Tier 4 model consists of proactive screening, care coordination, in-school outpatient therapy, and wraparound services.
- There are several forms of proactive screening and identification practices: SEL competency screening, SEBFS screening, mental health disorder screening, and gatekeeper training.
- Care coordination streamlines mental health referrals and can be implemented through an onsite or hotline model.
- In-school outpatient therapy improves access to outpatient care for students and can be conducted onsite or via teletherapy for some age groups.
- Wraparound mental health services bring school mental health services into the community and the home. A Master's level can work independently or can be paired with a therapeutic mentor and/or a family therapist to provide support to students and their families.

What's Next?

Having a firm understanding of the advantages of implementing a Tier 4 model provides a foundation for future planning. The ability to articulate these advantages will generate buy-in and excitement from critical stakeholders. Building this base of support is one of the main components of creating a successful Tier 4 implementation plan. This component, as well as other essential planning steps, will be outlined in detail in the next chapter.

10 Planning for Financial Sustainability

Throughout the book, we have shared a pathway to improve mental health services for students so that we can ensure that we meet their ever-changing needs. This vision of services requires identified and dedicated resources to move from planning to action. Importantly, these resources should be sustainable so that the systems put into place can impact the overall scope of the mental health of students and not just serve in the short-term. This long-term planning will result in shifts in overall student mental health and positively impact your school and broader community.

With the ability to execute sustainable changes to the support systems for students comes long-term improvements in students' mental health. In this chapter, we will illustrate an approach to identifying opportunities and successfully procuring funding so that you can improve the comprehensive support around the mental health of your students in your school community. Exercising this approach will guide you in identifying resources in places and from sources you may have yet to consider.

Staffing for Sustainability

Public schools often do not have adequate resources to support the wide-ranging needs of their entire student population. Unfortunately, services to support students are often underfunded within budgets. These funding realities are difficult and often force leaders to choose one thing over another. This ongoing juggling of resources, realignment of priorities, and realities of effective budgeting often result in a reactive versus a proactive posture. The area of mental health programming is not immune, and these difficult decisions often result in a patchwork of uncoordinated or reactionary support for students, often without a plan for long-term sustainability.

It is important that we think about an alternative approach that prioritizes mental health support for students. This will allow us to move from a reactionary approach to a proactive and intentional one. If this is done well, it will improve support services for students, allow districts to avoid costs for underserved students, and continue to increase the level of support required. One important foundational effort to achieve this is to identify a specific member of your staff who carries primary responsibility to support the development of your collaboratively developed Action Plan.

This will likely be a very challenging task. If this position does not exist, your work will initially involve finding funding to support this additional role in your district. While adding administrative roles to any district can be fraught with objections, this is an essential element of the program's success.

This individual's guidance, leadership, and decision-making will stay focused on the mission to improve mental health support for students. This individual will have the time and focus to not only develop responsive programming for students but also focus on the critical aspect of sustainability of programming, which includes continuing to identify funding sources to support the established structures. As mentioned, for this endeavor to be successful, you must plan for a sustainable and long-lasting implementation of the supports.

If your district already has someone who occupies this role or a similar role, it is important to determine the alignment of responsibility and experience. An audit of the existing role will help to ensure that the focus, skills, and background align with your intentions around elevating student mental health support. This audit will provide important information about how that employee spends their time and on what tasks. This information will be essential to understand if the position within your district requires any adjustments or restructuring to increase the possibility of success.

In the current state of educational funding, adding a position may not be possible. If that is your reality, you must consider ways to elevate the planning and focus to ensure that student mental health issues are supported effectively within your district. Whatever your circumstance, this work will likely not gain traction without the deliberate identification of an existing or new staff member who will be responsible for coordinating this work and planning.

Searching for Resources

With a soundly developed plan, it is time to identify the resources that can be harnessed to implement it. This is no easy task, as the demands in schools and districts always outweigh available resources. It is helpful to consider categories of resources that could support your efforts. When considering resources, think about the potential opportunities as follows:

- Existing Resources
- Local Resources
- Regional Resources
- National Resources

This approach will allow you to consider expanding opportunities for support. Importantly, this is about you finding resources to fund your developed plans rather than developing plans to align with discovered resources. If you chase every grant opportunity connected to student mental health without the developed plan, you will likely further complicate the current uncoordinated and overlapping resources.

Developing and Nurturing Relationships

Before delving into potential sources of revenue to support this programming, we must consider relationships. Like many things, success will be connected to the relationships you have developed and nurtured as you begin planning. Do not discount the value of relationship building. Often, it is those with whom you have a strong relationship who will make introductions and share opportunities you were unaware of.

This is your responsibility and that of the identified leader within your district. You will both need to commit significant effort to building relationships. You are responsible for continuing to share the district's plan regarding student mental health, connecting with other organizations, and identifying potential funding opportunities. This will lead to opportunities for funding that will allow you to put your plans into action.

Another opportunity around relationship building is to take on some formal responsibilities within these other organizations. You may have the opportunity to sit on the board, act in an advisory capacity, or serve on a subcommittee; your commitment to their organization will support their commitment to your district.

Existing Resources

Local resources are those that can be found within your district and your town or city. Often overlooked, local resources can be gained by reallocating existing funds or through the identification and access to other revenue streams.

Operating Budget

Perhaps the most logical starting point is with the operating budget. A district's operating budget is typically millions of dollars and funds much of the programming for the district. As you know, developing an operational budget is a statement of your district's priorities. As we have seen, student mental health issues have grown both in frequency and intensity, as discussed in earlier chapters. It is vital to identify where support for student mental health will fit within the typical funding for your district.

As you prepare for the development of the budget, you should think about the foundational supports of the program that are essential to be funded through that budget. Most district operating budgets have historically funded school counselors, perhaps social workers, and other clinicians. As discussed earlier, effective coordination is an important foundational support for the ongoing development of a comprehensive suite of mental health supports for students.

As the budget reflects district priorities, the budget development must make room for these priorities. While receiving additional fiscal resources for your planned mental health support may not be possible, reallocating current funds is possible. This review will require a deep interrogation of the activities and programs the operating budget supports.

As you begin a deep dive into the operating budget, and in anticipation of planning, it is helpful to adopt a framework to determine the relative value of those positions and programs funded by the budget. Adopting a questioning framework will help you and your team delve into the intended and actual impact of previous decisions around priorities. This approach will prevent you from focusing on pet projects, traditional programs, or exceptional personnel, even when the outcome differs from what is needed and/or anticipated.

The purpose, of course, is to identify funding for the mental health support plan that you have created. Some possible questions as you review each position and program within your district include the following:

- Does the position/program continue to live up to the district's vision?
- Is this position/program living up to the promise when implemented?
- Is the position/program successful? If so, what evidence are you relying on?
- Are any positions/programs duplicates and unnecessary?
- Can you scale back or modify the position/program without sacrificing impact?
- Do all of these have the desired impact?
- Are any positions/programs duplicative?
- Are your resources being used to leverage the MTSS model?
- Are there responsibilities that can be offloaded to non-salaried supports?

Assessing the effectiveness of positions or programs is necessary to find room for a comprehensive approach to mental health support. Doing so will help identify areas where budgetary adjustments can be made while preserving the most valuable elements of the educational experience and ensuring the district's overall mission is still being met.

Community Partner Spotlight: Effective School Solutions

Effective School Solutions (ESS) partners with school districts to help them implement in-person mental health and behavioral support programs, particularly focused on the needs of students with the highest acuity (e.g., Tier 3) challenges. ESS's comprehensive, clinically driven solutions are delivered directly in schools to effectively support the most acute student needs. Their programming has been proven to improve care, strengthen outcomes, address trauma, and keep students in their home districts.

ESS recognizes that to make meaningful changes to a district's mental health care programming, districts must first have a clear understanding of their current strengths and weaknesses, a focused vision for improvement, as well as proper policies, procedures, protocols, and tools to deliver high-quality clinical care. ESS can help districts analyze their current school-based mental health programs and provide recommendations on how to improve their mental health plans while building internal capacity to put their Multi-Tiered Systems of Support (MTSS) into practice.

ESS offers clinical programs that have been uniquely designed as a "symphony" of interventions working together to provide a powerful level of care for students with the most intensive mental health needs. All interventions used in the ESS therapeutic care model have a strong basis in research. Clinicians leverage proven protocols to effectively support at-risk students, with clinical supervision and risk management oversight provided to ensure program fidelity and impact. ESS programming has undergone an independent review conducted by the esteemed Yale Child Study Center. As a leader in child psychology and education, the Yale Child Study Center's validation underscores ESS programming's efficacy and reliability. This research corroborated ESS's impact on academic performance, discipline rates, and student attendance, as well as on higher levels of care referrals and therapeutic outplacements.

Creating a sustainable approach to funding comprehensive mental health services is crucial for ongoing student support. ESS's school-based mental health and behavioral support programs reduce the necessity and expenses associated with therapeutic outplacements, ensuring efficient use of resources while providing quality care within the school environment. ESS helps districts identify available funding sources for mental and behavioral health services. They also provide guidance on evaluating the effectiveness of therapeutic programs in terms of student outcomes and cost efficiency, ensuring the longevity of mental health initiatives.

Local and City/Town Resources

Another opportunity to gain additional funding is through local resources. Each community is unique, with structures and processes for support based on the community's needs. With that understanding, how might you leverage local resources to support components of your mental health support plan for students? Below are some possible partnerships and funding for your mental health support.

Town/City Supports

The children in your district are residents of your community. Although you may often consider support for your students as something that happens only through the district, it is essential to remember that there is broad community interest in supporting these students. You will be better poised to identify potential partnership opportunities with that shared understanding and responsibility. These partnerships should lead to increased funding opportunities to implement your developed plan.

For example, all communities are served by emergency services (e.g., police and fire departments). Often, these agencies have structures in place or access to resources to support the community's population. Improving awareness of their structures will help the district's understanding of where your agencies may partner to broaden support for school-aged children. Your local police department may employ a social worker to accompany officers on calls. Your local fire department may have resources and an interest in funding a community-wide mental health referral support service to help reduce the number of calls to emergency services related to mental health challenges. These partnerships will provide mutual benefit to the school district as well as the broader municipality.

In addition to direct support from other municipal agencies, it is also suggested that you review funding for your municipality. As you engage in this review, you are trying to identify other opportunities to access existing programs and/or funding. Schedule meetings with other town or city department heads to discuss your plan to improve student services and ask for their support in identifying potential partnership opportunities.

One example may be the ability of your district to become a recognized provider by state and private health insurance agencies. While an arduous and difficult process, gaining accreditation and recognition as a provider will allow the district to directly bill health insurers and receive payments to help provide sustainable funding for the staffing needs in the district. There are districts that have successfully adopted this approach, which has provided ongoing resources. There are state-to-state differences in the process of implementing this approach that need to be explored.

Beyond municipal agencies, you will find a wide range of support organizations within your community. These include parent-teacher organizations, youth sports organizations, scouting, etc. The stated goal of these organizations is to support youth within the community. If you ensure that leaders in these organizations know your Action Plan, partnership opportunities will develop.

There are also organizations within your community with the purpose of giving back and doing good. Organizations like the Rotary Club, Lions Club, Freemasons, and Kiwanis Club often are predicated on service and support. The Kiwanis Club, for example, has a stated mission: "Kiwanis is a global organization of volunteers dedicated to improving the world one child and one community at a time. Kiwanis will positively influence communities worldwide—so that one day, all children will wake up in communities that believe in them, nurture them, and provide the support they need to thrive."[1]

Building connections with these organizations and ensuring that leaders understand your Action Plan and how they might help provide you with opportunities to access previously unknown resources. Your ability to clearly articulate your plan, the anticipated benefits, and the overall impact will ignite excitement within these organizations to identify methods to provide support.

Local Health Agencies

Another area of potential support is local health agencies. In your community or within your area, many health organizations likely strive to support the community's health needs. For too long, these agencies and schools have not connected to identify opportunities to partner in this work. Often, these agencies have access to resources and expertise that are available to schools. This expertise and resources may be accessed through a variety of partnership opportunities. It is time to work more effectively together to engage the level of support necessary for students to succeed. Organizations to reach out to and discuss partnership opportunities:

- Community Mental Health Agencies
- Private Mental Health Practices

- Hospitals
- Nonprofits

Initiating a partnership requires intentionality. It begins with you reaching out and taking an interest in the organization—learning about who they are, their mission, and where the overlaps of purpose exist. In the early development of these relationships, think about how you can support their interests. Supporting their interests could include offering to share information about their services to the school community through typical communication channels. Or could result in direct referrals from the district to these organizations.

The reality is you will only know once you begin to explore. As you start your planning, you should develop a comprehensive list of these agencies. Once you have identified the agencies and the key players, plan a listening tour to learn more about the free and paid resources within or near your community.

National Organizations and Governmental Agencies

There is growing concern about student mental health issues and access. As a result, an increasing amount of effort and funding is being directed to support local agencies in addressing these issues. Below are some potential partnership and funding opportunities to investigate.

Federal Agencies

- Substance Abuse and Mental Health Services Administration (SAMHSA): (https://www.samhsa.gov/grants)
- US Department of Education (https://www.ed.gov/fund/grant/find/edlite-forecast.html)
- Centers for Disease Control and Prevention (CDC) (https://www.cdc.gov/funding/)
- National Institute of Mental Health (https://www.nimh.nih.gov/funding/index.shtml)

Private Foundations

- The Jed Foundation: The Jed Foundation focuses on promoting emotional health and preventing suicide among college and university students, but it also support initiatives in K-12 schools. (https://www.jedfoundation.org/grants/)
- The Hackett Family Foundation: This foundation supports programs that address mental health and wellness in schools, including funding for counseling services and mental health education. (https://www.hackettfamilyfoundation.org/grantmaking)
- The Robert Wood Johnson Foundation: While primarily focused on health and healthcare, RWJF occasionally funds projects to improve mental health outcomes for children and adolescents, including those in educational settings. (https://www.rwjf.org/en/how-we-work/grants.html)
- The Bill & Melinda Gates Foundation supports various education-related initiatives, including those that address student mental health and well-being in schools. (https://www.gatesfoundation.org/What-We-Do/Global-Development/Education)
- The Mental Health Foundation funds projects and programs to promote mental health awareness and support, including initiatives targeting schools and youth.(https://www.mentalhealth.org.uk/what-we-do/research/our-research-grants)

Seed Grants

Another opportunity to support funding your plans is to consider seed grants. These relatively small dollar grants may provide you with an opportunity to demonstrate effectiveness in a particular area before committing additional dollars. Seed grants can also help fund precursor work or planning that may lead to great opportunities. For example, some seed funding may allow you to hire a grant writer to go after more significant funding.

Finding funding for your Action Plan will take significant time and effort. A key element of your success is connected to your Action Plan and how you can leverage that plan to ignite excitement from individuals and organizations. The partnerships you develop will be vital in implementing your Action Plan.

Key Takeaways

- Identifying one staff member to coordinate district-wide mental health support is critical to the success of Tier 4 program integration.
- Numerous funding opportunities exist for every district, including internal, local, regional, and national resources.
- Building successful relationships is vital to funding a sustainable Tier 4 program.
- Seed grant funding can be used to demonstrate the impact of a Tier 4 program, which can help pave the way for sustainable funding.

What's Next?

At this point in the book, you should have a firm grasp of the advantages of integrating the MTSS Tier 4 model, how to plan a Tier 4 program, and how to access funds to launch and sustain a Tier 4 program. In the next chapter, we will provide examples of multiple configurations of a Tier 4 program. Our hope is that these examples help you find the model that is the best fit for your district at this time.

11 MTSS Tier 4 Model Examples

Conceptualizing the impact that a Tier 4 model can have on students, the components of the model, and potential funding sources are foundational understandings for any school district looking to support student mental health more effectively. However, moving the idea of a Tier 4 model from concept to implementation is best accomplished by the district/school leader visualizing what initial form of the model will work best in their district. To expedite this process, we've provided several examples of Tier 4 program configurations within this chapter. Before considering the Tier 4 program examples, we recommend mapping out some key factors about your district to provide the necessary context to visualize the initial Tier 4 model configuration that will work best for your district. We'd recommend considering your "initial" time period to be one to three years. To do so, please take a moment to answer the following questions:

What are your most under-addressed student mental health needs?

- Care coordination
- Access to outpatient therapy for all students
- Access to outpatient therapy for students who are publicly insured
- Family support (i.e., family therapy, social services, parent mentoring)
- Student mentoring
- Other _____

What internal resources are currently available to your most under-addressed student mental health needs?

- School social workers
- School adjustment counselors
- School psychologist
- School counselor/guidance counselor
- Dedicated care coordinator or subscription service
- Other _____

What community resources are currently available to your most under-addressed student mental health needs?

- Community mental health agencies
- Local outpatient therapists
- Local care coordination services
- State agencies/programs
- Municipal agencies/programs
- Other _____

What financial resources are available to your most under-addressed student mental health needs?

- Funds from the operating budget
- Grant funds
- State funding
- Municipal funding
- Other _____

What amount of funding will likely be available to initiate a Tier 4 program in the next one to three years?

- $0
- $5,000–$20,000
- $20,000–$50,000
- $50,000–$100,000
- $100,000+

After noting your current needs, resources, and potential budget, you are now well-equipped to consider the Tier 4 program examples, which should help you envision your district's starting point. What you will not see addressed within these examples is student screening tools. Student screening should be the foundation of any Tier 4 program, so we assume that each district within these examples has already established a screening process. After reading all the examples, we'll use reflection questions to prompt you to begin the mental construction of your district's Tier 4 program.

Case Example #1: Lakeside Public Schools

District size: 2,500 students, one lower elementary school, one upper elementary school, one middle school, and one high school

Internal mental health supports: Five adjustment/social workers, four psychologists, and seven guidance counselors.

Community mental health supports: Several outpatient mental health providers who accept primarily commercial insurance, and a mental health community agency that provides outpatient support for publicly insured students but has limited availability.

Most under-addressed student mental health needs: Lakeside Schools has invested heavily in their internal mental health staff, which gives them a counselor-to-student ratio that is higher than the national recommendations. However, this increase in internal staff has yet to yield the expected returns. Due to a lack of local outpatient providers and an increase in the prevalence of student mental health needs, school counselors spend much of their time trying to coordinate outpatient care. They typically spend over an hour and a half each school day on the phone with parents, clinicians, and insurance companies to find open appointments for their students. This gives them limited time to address student SEL needs across MTSS tiers one through three. Additionally, this tedious work impacts counseling morale and has resulted in staff turnover. Frustrated by the lack of impact on the investment in counseling services, the district administration decided to address this student need by adding a Tier 4 program.

Initial budget to launch a Tier 4 program: Due to several unanticipated retirements, resulting in a budget surplus, Lakeside has been able to carve out $30,000 to launch a Tier 4 program.

Tier 4 program approach: Having identified the most under-addressed student mental health care need as care coordination, the district administration meets with the school counseling team to seek a deeper understanding of the need. From this meeting, the administrative team was able to identify two main concerns. The first is a need for dedicated care coordination.

When school counselors attempt to find outpatient support for students, they call local clinicians they know or search for providers on psychologytoday.com; from their admission, neither approach is particularly effective or efficient.

Second, the community mental health agency that provides services for students who are publicly insured has a waitlist that is six months long, meaning that often, students go nearly an entire school year before having their initial appointment with a provider.

With this information in hand, the Lakeside team looks for partners to help them meet this need while staying within their budget. To address the care coordination concern, Lakeside partners with a care coordination service that will support all K-12 students, their families, and the Lakeside staff and their families. Parents can create a care coordination request, or the counselor can initiate the request, after which the care coordination team connects with the family, schedules an initial appointment, and follows up with the family to make sure the provider is a good fit. This service will cost Lakeside $8,000 for twelve months.

To better support publicly insured students in need of outpatient services, Lakeside will partner with a teletherapy group. The teletherapy group accepts all forms of insurance and guarantees an initial appointment within two weeks of the referral. Lakeside purchased fifty referrals to this service as part of a twelve-month contract. Due to the cap on referrals, the Lakeside team plans to primarily use their referrals for publicly insured students. The contract signed with the teletherapy company is for $20,000.

Outcomes: Revisiting Lakeside Schools a year later, we see a much-improved student and counselor experience. The school counseling team now spends an average of less than thirty minutes per day coordinating outpatient services (down from ninety minutes), which has freed them up to deliver Tier 1 SEL education and Tier 2 small group counseling sessions, neither of which were taking place prior to the addition of the Tier 4 program.

Additionally, publicly insured students saw their wait times for outpatient services cut down from six months to less than two weeks. This has resulted in these students having improved attendance and allowed school counselors to spend much less time in crisis management with this population of students. As a result of a $30,000 investment, much less than adding another school counselor, in a Tier 4 program, Lakeside has seen an improvement in student well-being and staff morale, and their school counseling team is now impacting the entire student population through MTSS Tiers 1 and 2.

Community Partner Spotlight: Cartwheel

Cartwheel is the trusted mental health partner to schools, delivering rapid access to care for students and helping districts build comprehensive support systems that catch kids before they fall. Their evidence-based model is designed specifically around the school ecosystem, enabling districts to expand access to care, increase staff capacity, strengthen family engagement, and track meaningful outcomes. Through our diverse network of licensed therapists and child psychiatrists, we ensure culturally responsive, affordable care for all students—including those with Medicaid or without insurance.

Recognizing these systemic challenges, Cartwheel developed a model that addresses four common gaps in care: student access, staff capacity and training, family engagement, and data collection. The access gap reflects students' limited ability to connect with appropriate care, while capacity constraints prevent district teams from managing care delivery at scale. Family engagement barriers often result in limited understanding and participation in the care process, and inadequate data collection systems make it difficult to assess program impact, guide improvements, and thus make the case for increased budget allocation in the area of student mental health. These gaps, while distinct, create a compounding effect that can significantly impair a district's ability to deliver effective mental health support.

To bridge these gaps, Cartwheel operates as a comprehensive virtual mental health clinic that employs diverse therapists, psychiatrists, and nurse practitioners who can provide a full spectrum of services. The virtual delivery model dramatically reduces access barriers by offering year-round care from 8:00 a.m. to 8:00 p.m., six days a week, in over fifteen languages. Clinical Program Managers work directly with district administrators, providing crucial consultation on program utilization and clinical oversight. This partnership ensures that districts can effectively manage and scale their mental health support without overtaxing internal resources and budgets.

Beyond direct clinical services, Cartwheel has developed a multi-layered approach to family engagement and program monitoring. Care Coordinators serve as dedicated advocates, working directly with families to navigate the care journey and ensure students not only start but complete their plans of care. The program offers regular family webinars and resources designed to empower parents as active partners in their child's mental health care. Additionally, Cartwheel's platform provides districts with real-time visibility into both individual student progress and aggregate program outcomes, enabling data-driven decision-making and continuous program improvement. This comprehensive approach ensures that mental health support remains coordinated, measurable, and aligned with educational goals.

The effectiveness of this reimagined approach is evident in the outcomes. While traditional models often involve months-long waiting lists, Cartwheel connects students with providers within seven to ten days for both therapy and psychiatric care. The program achieves a 75 percent first-session completion rate—a significant increase over the 20 percent to 57 percent found in research—and students typically engage in ten to twelve sessions.

Most importantly, 93 percent of students who work with Cartwheel show clinically significant improvement in anxiety and depression, with an average improvement of five points on GAD-7 and PHQ-8 scales. With a 98 percent district renewal rate and 90 percent parent recommendation rate, the model demonstrates both its effectiveness and sustainability in supporting comprehensive student mental health care. As districts look beyond temporary funding sources like ESSER, Cartwheel's approach offers a blueprint for sustainable, effective mental health support that truly meets the scale and complexity of student needs.

Case Example #2: Riverbend Area School District

District size: 1,225 students, one elementary school, one middle school, one high school

Internal mental health supports: two guidance counselors, one adjustment counselor, one social worker, and one psychologist.

Community mental health supports: Riverbend Area Schools is a regional district serving several rural towns. Due to the school district's geographic location, the closest pediatric mental health providers are located over an hour away. There are county youth and family services, but again, these services require an hour's drive to access.

Most under-addressed student mental health needs: The most under-addressed student mental health need at the Riverbend Schools is outpatient services for students with depression and anxiety. This population finds it difficult to secure outpatient therapy due to the lack of local providers. If a student is lucky enough to get an appointment with the closest provider, seventy minutes away, they also need a parent or guardian willing to drive them back and forth to this appointment each week. Although teletherapy has provided additional services for students in grades 7–12, younger students or students who need in-person therapy often need to wait as long as ten to twelve months to be seen. This lack of local providers has greatly impacted Riverbend's school counseling department.

Due to limited outpatient services, most of Riverbend's school counselors' time is spent providing individual counseling sessions. The counselors serve students with and without IEPs who need individual support but cannot access it within the community. As a result, there is limited time for Tier 2 group counseling and no Tier 1 SEL programming delivered by the school counseling team. With the likelihood of local outpatient services expanding in the near future being slim to none and no money within the school budget to add school counseling staff, the Riverbend administration team has decided to explore opportunities for a Tier 4 program.

Initial budget to launch a Tier 4 program: Riverbend is in a budget deficit and will not receive additional municipal or state aid next year. This leaves it with a total budget of $0 to launch a Tier 4 program.

Tier 4 program approach: With a clear understanding of the need they are trying to address, expanding access to outpatient services, and how much money they have to spend $0, the Riverbend administrative team conducts a community resource assessment. The result of the assessment indicates two glimmers of hope. There is a cluster of behavioral health providers that reside just over an hour from their school district, and there is a regional branch of a state university that is also situated just over an hour away from their campus.

The administrative team calls these providers and the university's academic affairs department to explain their needs and request meetings to explore collaboration. A few weeks later, Riverbend's superintendent and director of student services met with the university's president and the executive director of a pediatric mental health agency and walked away with two partnerships.

The Riverbend team explained the challenges of accessing mental health services to the executive director of the pediatric mental health agency, who in kind explained the difficulties of filling their pediatric outpatient therapist's schedule during school hours. To address both these challenges, Riverbend and the pediatric mental health agency agreed to have outpatient therapists conduct sessions during the school day within Riverbend's schools.

As long as the therapist's schedules were full each day, the agency would provide therapists at Riverbend's schools three days a week. Additionally, Riverbend agreed to help the local branch of the state university find students pursuing degrees in education or psychology with internships within their schools. In reciprocation, the university would help to place graduate school counseling students, along with a licensed clinician, in their schools twice a week to provide outpatient therapy sessions. Although these partnerships required Riverbend to provide space for therapeutic sessions, there were no direct costs associated with the launch of this Tier 4 program.

Outcomes: The efforts of the Riverbend team have paid significant dividends for their students and counselors. Students used to wait nearly a year, and families would have to endure a two-hour round-trip drive to access in-person outpatient mental health services. Now, students are typically seen by therapists during the school day, two to four weeks after a referral is made. This increase in access has helped to improve student attendance and academic performance.

Additionally, school counselors are no longer spending most of their time providing individual counseling sessions. This change in scheduling has freed them up to provide Tier 2 group counseling sessions and Tier 1 push-in SEL lessons. Of course, a time investment was made in establishing and maintaining collaborative relationships with the community mental health agency and university. Still, Riverbend was able to achieve these outcomes without spending any additional funds from its operating budget.

Case Example #3: Cedar Ridge Local School District

District size: with 23,300 students, seventeen elementary schools, six middle schools, and four high schools

Internal mental health supports: twenty-seven social workers, twenty-seven guidance counselors, and thirty psychologists.

Community mental health supports: Cedar Ridge is a rapidly growing suburban school district. To meet the needs of their growing student population, they have invested heavily in school counseling staff and community partnerships. Along with a growth in the student population, the Cedar Ridge area has seen a boom in its healthcare industry. This has made pediatric mental health services widely available and allowed Cedar Ridge to establish a Tier 4 in-school outpatient program in each high school.

Most under-addressed student mental health needs: Cedar Ridge feels great about how they've built up their internal counseling team and established community mental health partnerships to meet the rising student mental health needs. However, there is still an under-addressed student mental health needs, which is family support. Although Cedar Ridge Schools and the local healthcare agencies employ numerous social workers, they are all bound to an establishment: the school social workers to their respective buildings (and school hours) and the healthcare social workers to their outpatient clinics.

This structure has left a gap in care connected to family support and social services. Undeserving families' needs has led to increased rates of chronic absenteeism, high rates of school nursing visits, and behavioral incidents linked to the theft of food in the cafeteria. The Cedar Ridge administrative team plans to expand its Tier 4 model to include wraparound mental health services to address this gap.

Initial budget to launch a Tier 4 program: As Cedar Ridge's student population rapidly increases, so does its budget, thanks to increased commercial and tax revenue. Equipped with $500,000, the Cedar Ridge team sets forward to design its Tier 4 wraparound program.

Tier 4 program approach: The Cedar Ridge team knows that they'd like to integrate a wraparound mental health program, but they are unsure of what configuration of staff to hire to meet the needs of their families. Thus, they issue a survey to their school counselors to better understand what services families are most in need of. Some of the survey results were surprising. The greatest needs are support with school avoidance, a lack of generalization of social and emotional skills used by students at home and within the community, and social assistance.

To address these needs, the Cedar Ridge team believes hiring four licensed independent clinical social workers (LICSW) and three therapeutic mentors would be best. The LICSWs and therapeutic mentors will be hired outside of the union contract so that they can work a variable schedule that will allow them to meet with students and families outside-of-school hours and within the home and community.

The LICSWs will help to coordinate social services and create plans to help families better address school avoidance. The therapeutic mentors will work under the license of the clinical social workers to provide student mentorship and work with them on building and generalizing social and emotional skills within the home and community. The therapeutic mentor will also support students and families in executing the plans created to address school avoidance. The Cedar Ridge team believes they can hire the LICSWs for an average salary of $90,000 and the therapeutic mentors at an average salary of $45,000, which would come out to a total cost of $495,000.

Outcomes: After launching the Tier 4 wraparound program one year ago, Cedar Ridge experienced several positive outcomes. Most notably, rates of chronic absenteeism K-12 dropped by over 10 percent. This decrease in absenteeism was a direct result of the LICSWs and therapeutic mentors working with families to help establish goals, routines, and expectations for students and parents/guardians around attending school each day.

Additionally, the LICSWs were able to coordinate specialists to help work with students and their families who were avoiding school due to anxiety. Cedar Ridge's nursing and counseling staff have also has seen a dramatic drop in students presenting with concerns around malnutrition, housing, and hygiene. Finally, Cedar Ridge conducts an annual student survey to measure school connectedness. The survey results indicated that the percentage of students who feel connected to an adult at school rose from 72 percent to 80 percent across the district in grades 6–12. Due to the program's immediate impact, Cedar Ridge plans to expand the wraparound program as funding becomes available.

What would your district's Tier 4 program example look like?

Imagine you were to write an example of a Tier 4 program launch or expansion similar to the examples provided above about your district. What would it look like? Before answering this question, please consider the answers you provided to the questions posed at the beginning of this chapter. The answers to these questions, along with the examples of how other school districts launched Tier 4 programs, should provide you with the information you need to visualize what your district's initial Tier 4 program could be like.

Key Takeaways

- Gaining an understanding of Tier 4 programs that vary in student need, internal and external supports, scale, and budget can help you envision what type of initial Tier 4 program would work best for the district.
- Tier 4 programs are meant to be constructed over time and do not have to be initiated with all components in place.
- Tier 4 programs should be built based on student needs and available resources and will likely expand over time.
- All districts, even those with limited or no funding available, can initiate a Tier 4 program.

What's Next?

The upcoming chapter will focus on taking action. Sometimes, acquiring the knowledge you need to make a systems change is the easy part. The final chapter of this book will be about taking the action necessary to make a change in your district or school.

12 A Call to Action

For decades, schools have been working to meet the mental health needs of students. School counselors and other school-based mental health staff have continued to work to find treatment and support for students. Despite these efforts, the increased needs of students have overwhelmed available resources. The result is that schools are working with those students who exhibit the most significant needs, often at the cost of undersupporting those students with lower-level needs. The effect of this is that an increasing number of students elevate to higher levels of need and unnecessarily suffer negative outcomes due to the shortcomings of the current system.

Schools must take immediate action to change this dynamic. Schools must intentionally review, plan, and implement expanded support for students. Schools can no longer wait for or rely on external support and a system that has not been able to meet the needs of students. To make this shift, schools need to change their mindsets and practices to take on an expanded responsibility around student mental health treatment. But how do they do that?

A Farewell to Traditional MTSS

The traditional MTSS model has served us well. As an organizing framework, it has provided schools with a way to conceptualize the needs of students—both academically and socially-emotionally. However, the three-tiered MTSS model is ill-equipped to frame and allow for the support of the mental health needs of today's youth. It was not built with an understanding of what the rise of social media and the pandemic were going to have on the mental health of today's students.

The solution is not to discard the MTSS model completely. It has most of what schools need. The important adjustment to add Tier 4 provides an expanded framework for planning and treatment of students' mental health needs.

The updating of the MTSS model to include Tier 4 allows schools to provide students with access to the mental health services they need. The adoption of this expanded model also changes the locus of control from community services to those that will be planned, coordinated, and/or implemented by schools. The expanded Tier 4 model has four pillars:

- Proactive screening
- Care coordination
- In-school outpatient/teletherapy services
- Wraparound supports

When implemented individually, these supports have been shown to increase access to mental health treatment and improve attendance and academic performance. When bundled as a system of offerings that constitutes a Tier 4 program, they have the potential to greatly benefit students, a school, and a district. By implementing a Tier 4 program, district leaders are setting their students up for success today and are well-positioning their schools for what lies ahead for school mental health.

What Lies Ahead for School Mental Health?

For years, the state of adolescent mental health and the ability of schools to respond to the overwhelming needs could be summarized as tenuous, at best. Many students did not have their needs met either in school or within the community. This circumstance was amplified and reached a breaking point during and in the aftermath of the Covid-19 pandemic.

There are some positive signs that we have reached the peak need and that the tide might be approaching a turning point. Markers such as the recent Surgeon General's report,[1] the recognition of the harmful effects of cell phones in schools, the development of artificial intelligence (AI) tools to support school counselors, and a movement to broaden school mental health service reimbursement may be previewing better times ahead.

Recently, the Surgeon General has elevated the level of concern and enacted several initiatives to support child mental health, particularly emphasizing the importance of addressing the mental health crisis among youth. This includes issuing advisories that highlight the impact of social media on children, promoting mental health awareness, and calling for increased access to mental health services in schools.[2]

Additionally, there have been efforts to encourage community-based programs and resources aimed at supporting families and providing children with the tools they need for emotional resilience. These actions reflect a growing recognition by the highest-ranking government officials in the United States of the critical need for mental health support in the wake of increasing challenges faced by young people. This recognition of the student's mental health needs and its connection to mobile devices and social media use is getting a great deal of attention both in Western Europe and the United States.

An increased number of developed countries are recognizing the connection between smartphone use and mental health outcomes. Some of the first countries that moved to large-scale smartphone bans in schools are beginning to report the positive effects on student well-being. A study published by the Norwegian Institute of Public Health showed that school smartphone bans significantly decreased psychological symptoms, decreased bullying, and positively impacted academics.[3] These findings have led to several other European countries banning cell phone use in schools, including the Netherlands, Hungary, France, Belgium, Italy, and Greece.

Additionally, in the United States, states like Florida, Indiana, Louisiana, South Carolina, and California have enacted legislation regarding cell phone use in schools, with more states being added regularly. Certainly, the public health pursuits around cell phone bans in schools and the attention of the Surgeon General will only have a positive impact on student mental health, but these actions are set up to produce long-term results. In the more immediate future, the high volume of student mental health needs and a lack of pediatric mental health providers still very much exist. One way innovators are seeking to solve this problem is through the use of generative AI.[4]

Generative AI refers to computational techniques that can generate seemingly new, meaningful content such as text, images, or audio from drawing from existing data. Generative AI systems can be used to create new text, images, and video and can assist humans as intelligent question-answering systems[3]. At the time of publication, the exploration of use cases for generative AI is exploding. Schools are already starting to use generative AI applications to assist with curriculum development, class scheduling, and even IEP writing. These applications help teachers and administrators to be more efficient so that their valuable time can be used in other ways. A similar trend is also starting to emerge in the area of school counseling.

Although numerous, well-justified concerns exist regarding using AI to deliver direct, unchecked psychodynamic interventions to students, certain companies have developed AI applications that provide triangulated assistance to school counselors and their students, which adhere to evidence-based psychological frameworks and principles.[5] These therapeutic frameworks guide the conversational style of the AI assistant counselor and ensure that the responses are aligned with evidence-based practices, which are intended to enhance the AI assistant counselor's effectiveness, empathy, and reliability in real-world counseling scenarios.

This design allows the AI assistant counselor to work with students, with the oversight of a clinician, in a safe and appropriate manner. These types of applications offer great promise and may end up having a significant impact on the effectiveness and efficiency of school counseling interventions. The same could be said for the movement taking place in reimbursement for school mental health services.

As mentioned previously, funding school mental health services can be challenging. In recognition of this challenge, states like California have enacted legislation that allows school districts to bill both public and private insurance plans for behavioral health services. These billable services include all four pillars of the Tier 4 program: screening and assessment, care coordination, and treatment. This structure creates a sustainable funding source for Tier 4 school mental health services. As additional states adopt this type of legislation, school districts will be looking to hire staff and build structures that meet the requirements for reimbursement; we recommend putting your Tier 4 programming in place now to be ahead of the crowd.

While the future of child mental health support that schools may soon be able to provide looks promising, we are likely several years, if not decades, away from our pediatric mental health systems being able to meet the increased mental health needs of school-aged children. For this reason, we believe that schools must continue to explore structures that facilitate the treatment of child mental health needs so that they are able to fully engage in academics.

Closing

Student mental health issues continue to be a significant concern. While we may have already experienced the peak, the frequency and intensity of student mental health issues continue to require new approaches to ensure that the needs of all students are met. Schools must take a stronger role in supporting a comprehensive approach to student mental health challenges.

Adapting the traditional MTSS model by adding a Tier 4 provides an updated framework for schools to expand coordination and services for students. By doing so, the bottleneck that exists, where only those students with the most intense needs are being supported, will ease. This will allow schools to interrupt this current reality by providing mental health support for students at lower tiers of need. These supports are essential in ensuring that we are meeting the needs of students so that they can access an education that will positively impact their trajectory. The time for schools to act is now—by harnessing the full potential of Tier 4 to transform mental health support and ensure every student receives the care they need.

For additional resources and support, please visit: www.SELTier4.com.

Community Partner Spotlight Resources

Throughout this book, we have spotlighted potential partners and resources that help districts support their students' mental health needs. We've compiled those partners and SEL Tier 4 resources to facilitate your next steps, whether that is to continue learning or to collaborate with others to take action.

Effective School Solutions

Effective School Solutions partners with school districts to help them implement culturally inclusive mental health and behavioral support programs that improve care, strengthen outcomes, address trauma, and maintain students in their home district.

https://www.effectiveschoolsolutions.com/

Cartwheel Care

Cartwheel Care partners with K-12 school districts and delivers personalized support. Our licensed clinicians offer mental health care with no waitlists.

https://www.cartwheel.org/

kartoonEDU

kartoonEDU delivers durable, flexible, and affordable visual communications to public school districts of any size. It distills complex topics in public education into engaging, digestible media that districts can customize through a fee-for-license structure for a fraction of the price of commercial video production. By focusing on topics that are common to and not competitive between districts, kartoonEDU has helped more than sixty districts, and their leadership communicates their initiatives—from budgets to school safety.

kartoonedu.com, info@kartoonedu.com, (978) 261-7333

Care Solace

Care Solace is the mental health care coordination service of choice for K-12 school districts, higher education institutions, and municipalities.

https://www.caresolace.org Jed Foundation

The Jed Foundation is a nonprofit that protects emotional health and prevents suicide for our nation's teens and young adults, giving them the skills and support they need to thrive.

https://jedfoundation.org/

Notes

Chapter 2

1 Caetano, Carolina, Gregorio Caetano, and Eric Reed Nielsen. "Should children do more enrichment activities? Leveraging bunching to correct for endogeneity." (2020).

2 Pew Research Center. "Spring 2022 global attitudes survey. Q24&26. U.S. data from a survey conducted Jan 25-Feb 8, 2021." Accessed July 27, 2024. https://www.pewresearch.org/dataset/spring-2021-survey-data/.

3 Listernick, Zoe I., and Sherif M. Badawy. "Mental health implications of the COVID-19 pandemic among children and adolescents: What do we know so far?" *Pediatric Health, Medicine and Therapeutics* (2021): 543–49.

4 Johnston, Lloyd D., Patrick M. O'Malley, Richard A. Miech, Jerald G. Bachman, and John E. Schulenberg. "Monitoring the Future national survey results on drug use, 1975–2016: Overview, key findings on adolescent drug use." (2017).

5 Kalb, Luther G., Emma K. Stapp, Elizabeth D. Ballard, Calliope Holingue, Amy Keefer, and Anne Riley. "Trends in psychiatric emergency department visits among youth and young adults in the US." *Pediatrics* 143, no. 4 (2019).

6 Curtin, S. C. "State suicide rates among adolescents and young adults aged 10–24: United States, 2000–2018." *National Vital Statistics Reports* vol. 69, no. 11 (2020).

7 Racine, Nicole, Brae Anne McArthur, Jessica E. Cooke, Rachel Eirich, Jenney Zhu, and Sheri Madigan. "Global prevalence of depressive and anxiety symptoms in children and adolescents during COVID-19: A meta-analysis." *JAMA Pediatrics* 175, no. 11 (2021): 1142–50.

8 Yard, Ellen. "Emergency department visits for suspected suicide attempts among persons aged 12–25 years before and during the COVID-19 pandemic—United States, January 2019–May 2021." MMWR. Morbidity and mortality weekly report 70 (2021).

9. Hagan, Joseph F., Judth S. Shaw, and Paula M. Duncan. "Bright futures: Guidelines for health supervision of infants, children, and adolescents: Pocket guide." (2017).

10. Twenge, Jean M., Thomas E. Joiner, Megan L. Rogers, and Gabrielle N. Martin. "Increases in depressive symptoms, suicide-related outcomes, and suicide rates among US adolescents after 2010 and links to increased new media screen time." *Clinical Psychology Review* 6, no. 1 (2018): 3–17.

11. Riehm, Kira E., Kenneth A. Feder, Kayla N. Tormohlen, Rosa M. Crum, Andrea S. Young, Kerry M. Green, Lauren R. Pacek, Lareina N. La Flair, and Ramin Mojtabai. "Associations between time spent using social media and internalizing and externalizing problems among US youth." *JAMA Psychiatry* 76, no. 12 (2019): 1266–73. https://doi.org/10.1001/jamapsychiatry.2019.2325, increases in academic pressure

12. Kasser, T., and R. M. Ryan. "Further examining the American dream: Differential correlates of intrinsic and extrinsic goals." *Personality and Social Psychology Bulletin* 22, no. 3 (1996): 280–7.

13. Twenge, Jean M., Brittany Gentile, C. Nathan DeWall, Debbie Ma, Katharine Lacefield, and David R. Schurtz. "Birth cohort increases in psychopathology among young Americans, 1938–2007: A cross-temporal meta-analysis of the MMPI." *Clinical Psychology Review* 30, no. 2 (2010): 145–54.

14. Twenge, Jean M., and W. Keith Campbell. "Associations between screen time and lower psychological well-being among children and adolescents: Evidence from a population-based study." *Preventive Medicine Reports* 12 (2018): 271–83.

15. Vogels, E., R. Gelles-Watnick, and N. Massarat. "Teens, social media and technology 2022. Pew Research Center: Internet, science & tech. United States of America." Accessed September 19, 2204, https://www.pewresearch.org/internet/2022/08/10/teens- social-media-and-technology-2022.

16. Rideout, V., A. Peebles, S. Mann, and M. B. Robb. "Common Sense Census: Media use by tweens and teens, 2021." Accessed September 19, 2024 https://www.commonsensemedia.org/sites/default/files/research/report/8- 18-census-integ rated-report-final-web_0.pdf.

17. Riehm, Kira E., Kenneth A. Feder, Kayla N. Tormohlen, Rosa M. Crum, Andrea S. Young, Kerry M. Green, Lauren R. Pacek, Lareina N. La Flair, and Ramin Mojtabai. "Associations between time spent using social media and internalizing and externalizing problems among US youth." *JAMA Psychiatry* 76, no. 12 (2019): 1266–73.

18. Miech, Richard A., Lloyd D. Johnston, Jerald G. Bachman, Patrick M. O'Malley, John E. Schulenberg, and Megan E. Patrick. "Monitoring the Future: A

continuing study of American youth (8th- and 10th-grade surveys), 2021." Inter-university Consortium for Political and Social Research [distributor], 2022-10-31.

19 Orben, Amy, Andrew K. Przybylski, Sarah-Jayne Blakemore, and Rogier A. Kievit. "Windows of developmental sensitivity to social media." *Nature Communications* 13, no. 1 (2022): 1649.

20 Allcott, Hunt, Luca Braghieri, Sarah Eichmeyer, and Matthew Gentzkow. "The welfare effects of social media." *American Economic Review* 110, no. 3 (2020): 629–76.

21 Lamp, Sophia J., Alyssa Cugle, Aimee L. Silverman, M. Tené Thomas, Miriam Liss, and Mindy J. Erchull. "Picture perfect: The relationship between selfie behaviors, self-objectification, and depressive symptoms." *Sex Roles* 81 (2019): 704–12.

22 Rideout, V., and M. B. Robb. "Social media, social life: Teens reveal their experiences." Accessed September 19, 2024 Common Sense Media, https://www.commonsensemedia.org/sites/default/files/research/report/2018-social-media-social-life-executive-summary-web.pdf.

23 Wheaton, Anne G. "Short sleep duration among middle school and high school students—United States, 2015." *MMWR. Morbidity and Mortality Weekly Report* 67 (2018).

24 Alonzo, Rea, Junayd Hussain, Saverio Stranges, and Kelly K. Anderson. "Interplay between social media use, sleep quality, and mental health in youth: A systematic review." *Sleep Medicine Reviews* 56 (2021): 101414.

25 Telzer, Eva H., Diane Goldenberg, Andrew J. Fuligni, Matthew D. Lieberman, and Adriana Gálvan. "Sleep variability in adolescence is associated with altered brain development." *Developmental Cognitive Neuroscience* 14 (2015): 16–22.

26 Liu, Richard T., Stephanie J. Steele, Jessica L. Hamilton, Quyen BP Do, Kayla Furbish, Taylor A. Burke, Ashley P. Martinez, and Nimesha Gerlus. "Sleep and suicide: A systematic review and meta-analysis of longitudinal studies." *Clinical Psychology Review* 81 (2020): 101895.

27 Shochat, Tamar, Mairav Cohen-Zion, and Orna Tzischinsky. "Functional consequences of inadequate sleep in adolescents: A systematic review." *Sleep Medicine Reviews* 18, no. 1 (2014): 75–87.

28 Triana, Rike, Budi Anna Keliat, and Ni Made Dian Sulistiowati. "The relationship between self-esteem, family relationships and social support as the protective factors and adolescent mental health." *Humanities & Social Sciences Reviews* 7, no. 1 (2019): 41–7.

29 Beamish, Nicola Jane. "Parents' use of mobile computing devices, caregiving, and the social and emotional development of children: A systematic review and exploratory study of expert opinion." (2019).

30 Segool, Natasha Katherine. *Test anxiety associated with high-stakes testing among elementary school children: Prevalence, predictors, and relationship to student performance*. Michigan State University, 2009.

31 Gill, Brian P., and Steven L. Schlossman. "A nation at rest: The American way of homework." *Educational Evaluation and Policy Analysis* 25, no. 3 (2003): 319–37.

32 Scheb, Ryan. "Does homework work or hurt? A study on the effects of homework on mental health and academic performance." *Journal of Catholic Education* 26, no. 2 (2023): 130–43.

33 Holland, Melissa, McKenzie Courtney, James Vergara, Danielle McIntyre, Samantha Nix, Allison Marion, and Gagan Shergill. "Homework and children in grades 3–6: Purpose, policy and non-academic impact." In *Child & Youth Care Forum*, vol. 50, pp. 631–51. Springer US, 2021.

34 McMillan, Julia A., Marshall Land, and Laurel K. Leslie. "Pediatric residency education and the behavioral and mental health crisis: A call to action." *Pediatrics* 139, no. 1 (2017).

Chapter 3

1 McMillan, Julia A., Marshall Land, and Laurel K. Leslie. "Pediatric residency education and the behavioral and mental health crisis: A call to action." *Pediatrics* 139, no. 1 (2017).

2 "Accreditation Council for Graduate Medical Education (ACGME) Program requirements for graduate medical education in diagnostic pediatrics." Accreditation Council for Graduate Medical Education, Accessed September 19, 2024, https://www.acgme.org/globalassets/pfassets/reviewandcomment/320 _pediatrics_rc_022023.pdf.

3 Bunik, Maya, Ayelet Talmi, Brian Stafford, Brenda Beaty, Allison Kempe, Niramol Dhepyasuwan, and Janet R. Serwint. "Integrating mental health services in primary care continuity clinics: A national CORNET study." *Academic Pediatrics* 13, no. 6 (2013): 551–7.

4 McBain, R. K., A. Kofner, B. D. Stein, J. H. Cantor, W. B. Vogt, and H. Yu. (2019). "Growth and distribution of child psychiatrists in the United States: 2007–2016." *Pediatrics* 144, no. 6.

5 Axelson, D. (2019). "Meeting the demand for pediatric mental health care." *Pediatrics* 144, no. 6.

6 Chien, Alyna T., JoAnna Leyenaar, Marisa Tomaino, Steven Woloshin, Lindsey Leininger, Erin R. Barnett, Jennifer L. McLaren, and Ellen Meara. "Difficulty obtaining behavioral health services for children: A national survey of multi-physician practices." *The Annals of Family Medicine* 20, no. 1 (2022): 42–50.

7   Medicare Payment Advisory Commission. "Medicaid and CHIP payment and access commission." Data book: beneficiaries dually eligible for Medicare and Medicaid (2021).

8   Zhu, Jane M., Stephanie Renfro, Kelsey Watson, Ashmira Deshmukh, and K. John McConnell. "Medicaid reimbursement for psychiatric services: comparisons across states and with Medicare: Study compares Medicaid payments for mental health services across states and with Medicare." *Health Affairs* 42, no. 4 (2023): 556–65.

9   Lopez, Eric, Gretchen Jacobson, Tricia Neuman, and Larry Levitt. "How much more than Medicare do private insurers pay? A review of the literature." Kaiser Family Foundation. April 15, 2020. https://www.kff.org/medicare/issue-brief/how-much-more-than-medicare-do-private-insurers-pay-a-review-of-the-literature/.

10   Fengxian Li. "Impact of COVID-19 on the lives and mental health of children and adolescents." Frontiers in Public Health. October 18, 2022. Accessed August 2, 2024: https://pmc.ncbi.nlm.nih.gov/articles/PMC9623428/#:~:text=It%20was%20also%20reflected%20that,frustration%2C%20stress%2C%20and%20sadness.

11   EAB. "2023 voice of the superintendent: Key survey findings and crucial conversations for the year ahead." Accessed October 30, 2024. chrome-extension://efaidnbmnnnibpcajpcglclefindmkaj/https://pages.eab.com/rs/732-GKV-655/images/EAB%202023%20Voice%20of%20the%20Superintendent%20Survey%20Brief.pdf.

Chapter 4

1   National Center for Educational Statistics. "Over half of public schools report staffing and funding limit their efforts to effectively provide mental health services to students in need." May 9, 2024,https://nces.ed.gov/whatsnew/press_releases/5_9_2024.asp.

2   National Center for Educational Statistics. "Over half of public schools report staffing and funding limit their efforts to effectively provide mental health services to students in need." May 9, 2024,https://nces.ed.gov/whatsnew/press_releases/5_9_2024.asp.

3   Institute for Mental Health Policy. "Understanding the impact of mental health on academic performance." February 12, 2023, https://isminc.com/advisory

/publications/the-source/understanding-impact-mental-health-academic-performance.

4   Pew Research Center. "What's it like to be a teacher in America today?" April 4, 2024, https://www.pewresearch.org/social-trends/2024/04/04/whats-it-like-to-be-a-teacher-in-america-today/.

5   John Zogby Strategies. "Nationwide survey of parents of k-12 students & school administrators." November 2022, https://effectiveschoolsolutions.com/wp-content/uploads/2023/09/ESSZogbyNov2022PollFinalResults.pdf.

6   Kerfoot, Michael, Christos Panayiotopoulos, and Richard Harrington. "Social services and CAMHS: A national survey." *Child and Adolescent Mental Health* 9, no. 4 (2004): 162–7.

7   I-MTSS. Brief History of I-MTSS: "Major milestones toward an integrated framework." March 23, https://mtss.org/wp-content/uploads/2023/03/Major-Milestones-toward-I-MTSS-3.13.23.pdf.

Chapter 7

1   Green, Jennifer Greif, Katie A. McLaughlin, Margarita Alegría, E. Jane Costello, Michael J. Gruber, Kimberly Hoagwood, Philip J. Leaf, Serene Olin, Nancy A. Sampson, and Ronald C. Kessler. "School mental health resources and adolescent mental health service use." *Journal of the American Academy of Child & Adolescent Psychiatry* 52, no. 5 (2013): 501–10.

2   National Institute of Mental Health. "Children and mental health: Is this just a stage?" Accessed September 20, 2024. https://www.nimh.nih.gov/health/publications/children-and-mental-health.

3   National Center for School Mental Health. "School mental health quality guide: Screening." (2020).

4   National Institute of Mental Health. "Child and adolescent mental health." Accessed July 24, 2024. https://www.nimh.nih.gov/health/topics/child-and-adolescent-mental-health.

5   Center for Disease Control. Accessed July 24, 2024. https://wisqars.cdc.gov/

6   Singer, Jonathan B., Terri A. Erbacher, and Perri Rosen. "School-based suicide prevention: A framework for evidence-based practice." *School Mental Health* 11 (2019): 54–71.

7   American Psychological Association. "Children, youth, and families." Accessed July 24, 2024. https://www.apaservices.org/advocacy/issues/children-youth-families.

8. Agnafors, Sara, Mimmi Barmark, and Gunilla Sydsjö. "Mental health and academic performance: A study on selection and causation effects from childhood to early adulthood." *Social Psychiatry and Psychiatric Epidemiology* 56 (2021): 857–66.

9. Bertram, Rosalyn M., Jesse C. Suter, Eric J. Bruns, and Koren E. O'Rourke. "Implementation research and wraparound literature: Building a research agenda." *Journal of Child and Family Studies* 20 (2011): 713–25

10. Cox, K., Baker, D., & Wong, M. "Wraparound services in systems of care: How do the needs of children with serious emotional disturbance and their families impact program implementation?" *Journal of Child and Family Studies* 15, no. 4 (2006): 427–41.

11. Dore, M. M., and L. B. Alexander. "Preserving families at risk of child abuse and neglect: The role of the helping alliance." *Families in Society: The Journal of Contemporary Social Services* 20, no. 4 (1996): 349–61.

12. Rones, Michelle, and Kimberly Hoagwood. "School-based mental health services: A research review." *Clinical Child and Family Psychology Review* 3 (2000): 223–41.

13. Grossman, Jean Baldwin, and Joseph P. Tierney. "Does mentoring work? An impact study of the Big Brothers Big Sisters program." *Evaluation Review* 22, no. 3 (1998): 403–26.

14. Rhodes, J. E., R. Reddy, J. B. Grossman, and J. M. Lee. "Volunteer mentoring relationships with minority youth: An analysis of same- versus cross-race matches." *Journal of Primary Prevention* 26, no. 2 (2005): 129–45.

15. Herrera, Carla, David L. DuBois, and Jean Baldwin Grossman. "The role of risk: Mentoring experiences and outcomes for youth with varying risk profiles." Mdrc (2013).

16. National Alliance on Mental Illness. "Early intervention." Accessed July, 25, 2024. https://www.nami.org/Your-Journey/Kids-Teens-and-Young-Adults/Early-Intervention.

17. National Center for School Mental Health. "Comprehensive school mental health programs and absenteeism reduction." Accessed July 24, 2024. http://www.schoolmentalhealth.org/Resources/Foundations-of-School-Mental-Health/Comprehensive-School-Mental-Health-Systems/.

18. School Social Work Association of America. "In-home social work programs and student attendance." Accessed July 25, 2024. https://www.sswaa.org/school-social-work.

19. Herman, K. C., W. M. Reinke, A. M. Thompson, and R. Hawkings. "Reducing behavioral problems in early childhood through early intervention." *Journal of School Psychology* 79 (2020): 1–12.

20. National Alliance on Mental Illness. "Early intervention." Accessed July, 25, 2024. https://www.nami.org/Your-Journey/Kids-Teens-and-Young-Adults/Early-Intervention.
21. Child Mind Institute. "Family-based interventions." Accessed July 25, 2024. https://childmind.org/guide/parents-guide-to-problem-behavior/.
22. Centers for Disease Control and Prevention. "Mental health and academic achievement." Accessed July 25, 2024. https://www.cdc.gov/healthyschools/mentalhealth.htm.
23. Weist, M. D., and M. J. Furlong. "The role of school-based mental health services in enhancing academic achievement." *Journal of School Psychology* 52, no. 2 (2014): 133–45.
24. Mccance-Katz, Elinore. "Guidance to states and school systems on addressing mental health and substance use issues in schools." Accessed July 26, 2024. https://store.samhsa.gov/sites/default/files/pep19-school-guide.pdf.
25. National Association of Social Workers. "The role of social workers in supporting student achievement." Accessed July 25, 2024. https://www.socialworkers.org/Link/How-Social-Workers-Help.
26. Child Trends. "The impact of in-home social work services on academic performance." Accessed July 26, 2024. https://www.childtrends.org/publications/the-impact-of-in-home-social-work-services-on-academic-performance.
27. American Educational Research Association (AERA). "The effectiveness of comprehensive in-home social work programs on student test scores." *American Educational Research Journal* 57, no. 4 (2020): 1234–56.
28. Geelhoed, Elizabeth, Joelie Mandzufas, Phoebe George, Ken Strahan, Alison Duffield, Ian Li, and Donna Cross. "Long-term economic outcomes for interventions in early childhood: protocol for a systematic review." *BMJ Open* 10, no. 8 (2020): e036647.
29. Frank, Richard G., and Thomas G. McGuire. "Economics and mental health." *Handbook of Health Economics* 1 (2000): 893–954.
30. García, Emma, and Elaine Weiss. "Reducing and averting achievement gaps: Key findings from the report 'education inequalities at the school starting gate' and comprehensive strategies to mitigate early skills gaps." Economic Policy Institute (2017).

Chapter 9

1. Jellinek, Michael S., J. Michael Murphy, John Robinson, Anita Feins, Sharon Lamb, and Terrence Fenton. "Pediatric symptom checklist: Screening school-age

children for psychosocial dysfunction." *The Journal of Pediatrics* 112, no. 2 (1988): 201–9.
2. Birmaher, B., S. Khetarpal, D. Brent, M. Cully, L. Balach, J. Kaufman, and S. W. Neer. "The screen for child anxiety related emotional disorders (SCARED): Scale construction and psychometric characteristics." *Journal of the American Academy of Child & Adolescent Psychiatry* 36, no. 4 (1997): 545–53.

Chapter 10

1. Kiwanis International. "Kids need kiwanis." Accessed November 7, 2023. https://www.kiwanis.org/.

Chapter 12

1. Murthy, V. "Social media and youth mental health: The US Surgeon General's advisory; 2023." (2023): 07–16.
2. Murthy, V. "Social media and youth mental health: The US Surgeon General's advisory; 2023." (2023): 07–16.
3. Abrahamsson, Sara. "Smartphone bans, student outcomes and mental health." NHH Dept. of Economics Discussion Paper 01 (2024).
4. Feuerriegel, S., J. Hartmann, C. Janiesch, et al. "Generative AI." *Business & Information Systems Engineering* 66 (2024): 111–26. https://doi.org/10.1007/s12599-023-00834-7.
5. Hyopthetical AI. "Supercharge school counseling with AI." Accessed on October 7, 2024. https://www.hypothetical.school/.

About the Authors

Armand Pires, PhD, has served as a superintendent of schools in Massachusetts since 2015, bringing over two decades of diverse experience in education to his leadership. His career spans roles such as assistant superintendent, middle school principal, and educator at both middle and high school levels, providing him with a comprehensive understanding of educational systems.

Armand holds a Bachelor of Science degree, a Master of Public Health, and a PhD, and his research interests focus on leadership development, student mental health, and professional growth for educators. These passions align with his dedication to fostering supportive and effective learning environments. Armand's work reflects his belief in the transformative power of education and the critical importance of addressing the mental health needs of students.

Armand was also recognized as the 2025 Massachusetts Superintendent of the Year.

Ryan Sherman, DBH, has been the director of Wellness for Medway Schools since 2016. Over this time, he focused on bridging the gap between schools and the outpatient mental health care system. Before arriving in Medway, Ryan worked as a behavioral health provider at Massachusetts General Hospital. Ryan is the primary author of several peer-reviewed behavioral health research studies and a senior professor of social and emotional learning at Cambridge College. Dr. Sherman has been the recipient of the Massachusetts Interscholastic Athletic Association Wellness Coordinator of the Year and the Massachusetts General Hospital Innovation awards. For more information go to www.SELTier4.com.